THE HANDBOOK OF
STAGE COSTUME

Tina Bicât

THE HANDBOOK OF
STAGE COSTUME

First published in 2006 by
The Crowood Press Ltd
Ramsbury, Marlborough
Wiltshire SN8 2HR

www.crowood.com

© Tina Bicât 2006

British Library Cataloguing-in-Publication Data
A catalogue record for this book is available from the British Library.

ISBN 1 86126 807 6
EAN 978 1 86126 807 5

Dedication
Love, for Alexander and Becks, Polly and Lionel.

Acknowledgements
I would like to thank St Mary's College at Strawberry Hill for allowing me to reproduce the *Portrait of an
Unknown Girl* and the cartoon of The Right Honourable Chichester S. P. Fortescue. Also Adrian Morris,
Alan Leith, Alistair Milne, Amy Bicât, Chris Baldwin, Deborah Taylor, Gwyneth Powell, Jonathan
McDonnell, Mike Murnane, Nik Mackey, Robbie Jack, Robin Brodhurst and Robin Cottrell, and all the
actors and technicians in the photographs for their help. Thanks also to the drama students of St Mary's
College at Strawberry Hill for their interest and encouragement.

Designs, drawings and photos by the author unless otherwise stated.

Note: 'He' and 'she', 'him' and 'her', 'his' and 'her' are used throughout the book in an arbitrary
manner as both sexes work in all departments in theatres.

Frontispiece: *The Rock and Paint Show*. For Pegasus and Chipping Norton Theatre. Designer Jenny
Gaskin, music Barbara Gaskin and Dave Stewart. Photo: Jenny Gaskin

Cover photographs: copyright Robbie Jack
Front cover: Leslie Phillips (as Sir Sampson Legend) in *Lover for Lover* at Chichester Festival Theatre.
Back cover: Allison Cook (as Babette), Yvette Bonner (as Philippa) and Oliver Dumait (as Soldier)
in *Babette's Feast* at the Linbury Studio Theatre, Royal Opera House, Convent Garden.

Designed and edited by Focus Publishing,
11a St Botolph's Road,
Sevenoaks
Kent TN13 3AJ

Printed and bound in Singapore by Craft Print International

CONTENTS

1 THE MESSAGE OF COSTUME

Everybody understands costume. It might seem like a specialist subject and can become as complicated as anyone cares to make it, but the truth of the matter is that the clothes we choose to wear reflect the way we feel and the way we want others to feel about us. Our first impression of people we meet is likely to be influenced by their appearance. Costume has always been an essential ingredient of theatre performance because humans are so good at understanding the messages it gives. Before an actress opens her mouth, her elegant, beautifully fitted dress in supple satin has told a different tale from the loose, faded jeans and T-shirt of her co-star. A simple adjustment to the costume – a muddy hem and a torn shoulder seam on the pale satin, or a map sticking out of the jeans pocket and a rucksack on the back – enriches the audience's perception of the character they see on the stage.

Most children and quite a lot of adults enjoy dressing up. Wearing clothes that do not belong to everyday life can act as a passport to a style of behaviour that is not encouraged by everyday clothes. A small child can become a princess or a superhero with the help of a towel tied on as a cloak; adults are familiar with the confidence-building effect of clothes that feel right for the occasion – although a towel round the neck after the age of seven may not improve the confidence as much as a perfectly fitting and flattering outfit.

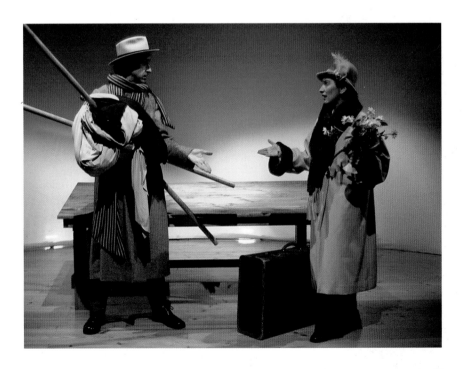

OPPOSITE: *Juliet Stevenson, Simon McBurney and members of the company in Théâtre de Complicité's production of The Caucasian Chalk Circle. Photo: Robbie Jack*

RIGHT: *Accessories and props give these simple costumes a sense of period and character. Photo: Mikel Saiz*

Everybody knows the misery of wearing clothes that feel wrong. This universal understanding gives the costume designer a head start; it means that it is probable that every sighted person in the audience understands the messages that he is signalling.

THE COSTUME DESIGNER AND THE COMPANY

The Actor and Costume

The best way to understand how important costume is to an actor is to watch the way an experienced performer behaves at a fitting in the Wardrobe or costume room. Their first concern is for the practicality of the costume. Does it allow them to move in the way they will need to move in performance? Will Romeo's doublet allow him enough freedom for the climb up to Juliet's balcony and will her nightdress remain virginally modest when she bends forward to help him over the railing? Performers are accustomed to coping with costumes that are heavy, hot and constricting; at the fitting the balance between the pictures the audience sees, and the ability of the actor to perform in the costume must be achieved.

Once the practicalities have been sorted out, the actor will begin to work, using the mirror as an audience. This is not vanity. Actors have to be confident of the picture they present so that they can forget their appearance and concentrate on the character they are playing. In order to do this, they have to feel right in their clothes. They have to have time to experiment in the costume; to see which actions would cause a frilled cuff to hide their expression from the upper circle, or what it will feel like when they draw their sword through the folds of their coat to attack the enemy. Even in the midst of a scene of high emotion or hysterical action, actors must be able to show their state of mind to the audience.

The Director and Costume

The way directors address the issues of costume can vary and depends both on their knowledge and interest in the subject and the power of their visual imagination. Some directors visualize the whole play in exact detail even before the first meeting with the designer; others have no clear visual picture to accompany their understanding of the characters. Some like the play to have been designed before the first read-through, so that the picture the play will present on the stage is clear in the mind of the whole company from the start; others prefer to work with the designer in rehearsal to create the costumes. Most hover between those two extremes.

Directors tend to choose to work with designers whose imagination and working practice complement, and balance with, their own. It can take some time to establish a creative and practical relationship and to build the vocabulary of understanding that leads to an easy exchange of ideas; once a successful partnership has been established the director/designer collaboration may be re-employed over and over again. The confidence and trust that develops between a designer and a director who work well together can release an exciting and powerful creativity, which exerts a strong influence over every aspect of production.

The Set Designer and Costume

In many cases, the same designer will create both set and costume and there will be no possibility of a clash in styles. Excellent communication is vital when the two are designed by different people. Tradition has created an unspoken agreement, based on practical necessity, that the set designer leads the process. The set is fixed, while the costumes move around, using it as a background. The parameters of the set are less flexible than those of the costume; it is usually constructed earlier and is often more expensive. Considerations dictated by the budget make it more difficult to make radical changes to the set than to the costume. Consequently, the colours and tones, and the general feeling of the pictures the audience sees onstage, will have been initiated by the set designer.

In more recent times, however, things have changed, led initially by the budget and demands of small-scale touring productions and work

Light-coloured costumes coloured by blue lighting. Photo: Robin Cottrell

devised and scripted through improvization and experiment in rehearsal. The setting for a play may be a very simple background, which is given life and colour by props and furniture. In such productions the costumes are thrown into high relief and become the clues that establish place and time in a way that the set would do in a more traditional production. This is an exciting stroke of luck for the costume designer today and makes the work even more creative, varied and exciting than it was in the past.

The Lighting Designer and Costume

In a film, the camera directs the viewer's eye to particular details; on a stage, the lighting, and the way it affects colour and texture, influences the audience's choice of what to look at. The power of light onstage is bumped up by the effect light has on the emotions. Most humans relax before the warm glow of a fire or candle, feel happier in sunshine and more prone to gloom in grey drizzle.

Look at your sleeve in ordinary indoor light and then look at it under the close beam of a light bulb. Note how the textures are enhanced, the colours leap into life, the highlights sharpen and the shadows have a new and powerful depth. Drama for the eyes and emotions. The actors and the lighting provide the magic that gives costumes theatrical life. Without it, costumes are dreary rags or, at best, merely everyday clothes. All this means that establishing a dialogue with the lighting designer is essential.

There is always too little time towards the final stage of any production. It is likely that the first time the costume designer sees the effect of the work of the lighting designer will be at the technical rehearsal. Time may be too short at that stage to change effects that do not work. The costume designer can help to avoid problems by providing colour swatches of the costumes and talking through the costume designs at an early meeting.

Costumes can give an impression of period and character without being historically accurate.
Photo: Robin Cottrell

ASPECTS OF COSTUME

Sound

Sound has an ability to conjure up places and memories. The sound costumes make when they move onstage is not heard unless the auditorium is small or the sound onstage is amplified. There does exist, particularly in more abstract, less naturalistic performance, or dance, the opportunity for a costume designer to play with the sound of a costume. It is easy to imagine the swishing, opulent sound of a stiff silk taffeta skirt, the percussion of tap shoes and the clank of metal armour. These sounds are all familiar. But think of dressing a sea nymph in skirts of shredded, rustling, plasticized paper – the sort of stuff that is used to wrap audio and computer equipment. Her movements would conjure the sound of the sea. Give a melodramatically sinister or comic butler a squeak or click in the heel of one shoe. A soundscape of possibility opens up if the script or the genre presents the opportunity to design costumes that give the audience an aural, as well as a visual, experience.

Getting the Message to the Audience

It is easy, in the passionate and busy business of creating a performance, to forget that the audience is the thing that makes it all possible. Otherwise, the product is an artistic experiment or a therapeutic experience for the actors and not a performance. The costume designer's main job is to use visual messages to give the audience a better understanding of the characters and their situation. There is a huge and delightful range of secondary games that costume can play with the audience: beautiful and exciting pictures, jokes and surprises, evocations of the past and future, airy flights of fancy, dense horror and magic with sound and light. But all of it must relate to and clarify the characters and the action onstage. Otherwise it becomes a self-indulgent designer's whim and will blur the audience's experience even if it delights their eyes. Balanced collaboration between director and designers creates the best possible experience for the audience.

Silhouette

Humans are very good at de-coding silhouettes. We've all been practising since we were babies and first looked up at our mother. Imagine you are coming out of the sea on a beach in the bright sunshine. The details of your group will be blurred by the bright light; your eyes too dazzled to distinguish the small patches of colour that are not skin. But the shape of the group will tell you where they are. The audience will use the silhouette of the costumes to understand your messages in much the same way.

What image comes into your mind when you think of a Victorian lady and gentleman? Probably the bell-shaped skirt, tight waist and bonnet of the woman and the top hat and straight, upright figure of the man. Try to imagine in the details of the picture and the image becomes less clear in your mind as the choice of possibilities of character and style open to you. Shadow puppetry has used this method to tell stories for thousands of years and perfected the telling of a complicated story in two-dimensional silhouettes.

Texture

The texture of a cloth governs its ability to reflect light. Look at a group of different fabrics together and notice the way they react to light directed on them. Texture onstage is not always what it seems. The rough calico of the penniless orphan's dress may be more clearly represented by an unevenly woven or open-weave silk that reflects the light in a way that makes the weave of the material obvious, and hangs in the floppy well-worn manner of old rags. Sometimes, cheap polyester satin, which does not crease, will be more effective, and look more expensive, than a pure silk satin whose creases are enhanced by the light. When choosing textures for costumes their reaction to light must always be considered, along with the way the cloth hangs when it falls naturally on the body. Brocade and damask give particularly clear examples of the way cloth reacts to light. The cloth may be of one single

Complicated messages can be decoded from a precise silhouette.
Photo: Mikel Saiz

11

colour and its pattern is created by the way it is woven. Certain parts, perhaps flowers, of the design are shiny, while the background is matt. This contrast, which uses two textures that react so differently in the light, will send the pattern of the cloth out over the footlights to the eyes of the audience with remarkable clarity. It is a useful tip when shopping, if you are not used to choosing material by texture, to carry a small, bright torch to mimic the effect of the stage-light and help your imagination.

The apparent weight of the cloth is controlled by its texture and again this is not always what it seems. The way the cloth is woven, as well as the yarn used in its manufacture, make it appear heavy or light when it is seen onstage. The manufacture of cloth is a huge and complicated subject but the technicalities are unimportant to the costume designer; it is what you see when you look at it, and the way it moves that count. Hold a

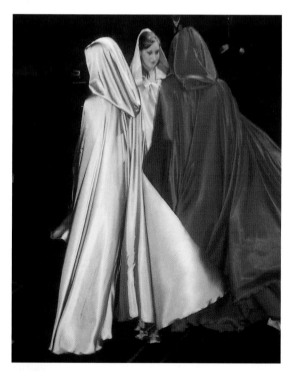

The drape of a fabric is apparent in the flow of these cloaks.

piece of cloth up by one corner or drape it over a chair and look at it from a distance. Wave it around. Blow it. Flop it up and down. Runkle it up and let it fall out of the creases. Waft it on the air. Swirl it about. Then you can ask yourself if it does what you want and feels appropriate to the character for whom you are designing. Never buy cloth without unrolling or unfolding an arm's length for experiment. If a shop owner objects to you doing this, don't go there again.

Contrast

Sew black buttons on a white shirt and they will show up clearly. Sew black buttons on a black shirt and they will hardly show up at all. This is an obvious example of an obvious contrast. But there are hundreds of occasions when you don't want costumes to have such an unsubtle contrast. Perhaps it is a funeral scene and everyone on the stage is dressed in black. Somehow you have to create differences of class, wealth, status, age and character, and the way you do it is by contrasting and combining textures. The thing to hold in your mind is the way that light behaves on different surfaces. Contrast two extremes: the diamond flash of a black sequin, which, despite its dark colour, absorbs no light and ricochets every ray of light that touches it back to watching eyes; and thick, black, felted wool, which has a softened surface that seems to suck up light and keeps it dense and matt in the rays of light. Picture that sequin on the woollen surface and imagine the effect of the contrast of their two textures. Sequins and felt are extremes. There are innumerable textures – which react in different ways. Look at a group of workers leaving their city office at the end of a working day and notice the range of texture in dark suits, ties, shoes, hair, coats, bags, briefcases. And then imagine how varied and visually exciting that all-black funeral scene could be.

Colour

Colour and the way we see it is inexplicable. No one can tell if the colour one person calls 'yellow' is the same as the colour seen by another. Despite the difficulty of talking about colours, there is no doubt that they have a powerful effect on the way we view the world. There are colours, such as blue, which are casually referred to as cold colours; but is it true? What about the hot blue of a Mediterranean sky? Red is associated with many different states, all of them stirring, but different: passion, anger, blood of course, violence, lust, self confidence, happiness. It is impossible to rely on colour to tell a story when people de-code it in such a variety of ways, but you can be sure that it will be noticed. The way the different colours are used together, and the power one colour has to change another when seen in the same eyeful, represents a study that goes on for ever.

There are all sorts of rules about colours that are supposed to look bad together but it is a great mistake to pay them any attention. It is not right to talk about 'blue' or 'red', for example, as just one colour. There are hundreds of different reds and blues and each one can be darker or lighter. Think of the difference between poppies and port and redcurrants and blood; red is not only a colour. It is about tone and texture and reflection. The blood seems full of absorbed pigment and the redcurrant reflects the light of the sky. A purplish red can be close to blue and the red of a nasturtium may seem saturated with hidden yellow. The same orange will seem to change its colour when seen against a bright blue sky and then against a red velvet tablecloth. Man and nature jumble colour all round us and there are endless opportunities, if we pay attention, to steal ideas from all these happy accidents.

Nature makes successful bunches of the most unlikely combinations of colours. The designer has to plan more strategically and create a picture onstage that may appear to be a chaos of colour, but will react harmoniously with light, and will enhance and not distract the people in the audience or confuse their understanding of the action.

HOW THE AUDIENCE SEES THE PICTURE

The costume designer does not produce pictures onstage for other costume designers or fashion historians. The audience is a creature with many minds and the best designs are those that trigger an understanding and response in every one of its members. Of course, a designer must be familiar with the clothes, accessories, manners and deportment of different historical periods, but an understanding of the characters they are dressing is just as important. And the designer must not only understand the characters onstage, but also the message the audience will derive from the way these characters look. In a 1930s play, you may dress a young man in a suit and accessories in the fashion of 1910 and assume it will make him look unfashionable and out of place. But there is little point – hardly anyone in the audience will remark the difference. However, if you make his trousers a little too short and his jacket a bit tight, they will notice and absorb the difference between his style and that of his friend in the perfectly fitting suit.

The audience only has one chance to see the pictures you put onstage. Some of them will take in every detail of the costumes and notice each shoelace and ruffle. Others will take in the whole of a scene in one visual sweep and respond to the general effect of the costumes rather than individual details. There will also be some to whom the things they see are much less important than the things they hear; they will scarcely notice the costumes at all. All these people and their different perceptions must be satisfied by your costume designs. Some of the best designs seem so natural and appropriate that they will hardly be noticed at all.

THE ROLE OF COSTUME IN PERFORMANCE

Setting a Period

Costume plays a primary role in leading the audience's understanding to the era when the action onstage is supposed to take place. Over the last fifty years, as television, video and films have become a part of the life of so many people, the methods a designer uses have changed dramatically. In the past it was a very occasional treat for most people to see a performance of a story. Today, as we flick the remote control, performed stories are as commonplace as the sound of cars.

This familiarity with seeing actors in costume – for even in the most naturalistic soap opera the actors are in a costume that has been designed for the character – has given every theatre audience an experience and understanding of costumes past and present. Before the advent of television costume drama, any long, full skirt on a woman or pair of tights and tunic on a man would tell the average member of the audience all they needed to understand from the costume about the period of the play. Any messages the costume gave had to be bold and obvious. Today the costume designer can be more subtle. The audience, familiar with costume drama on screen, can tell the difference between the Tudor tunic and the medieval one and the skirts of Jane Austen's women from the skirt of a Dickensian woman. They may not realize it, and might deny knowing anything about costume at all, but if you test with a silhouette figure many will recognize the time in history. Most will probably not connect it with a date, however, and will be more likely to associate it with a person, such a Henry VIII or Robin Hood, who will, in turn, conjure up a feeling of the era.

All this buried knowledge gives the designer more freedom to be subtle with colour, cut and accessories. And it is the cut and the accessories that alter the movement of actors and create the social life and manners of past times. The way a man moves in a full-skirted eighteenth-century coat, with sword and boots, suggests the time strongly, as does the particular way a woman will hold her body and flutter her fan when she is wearing the corseted bodice of the time. But we can still find an association of image in the confident maleness of the booted buccaneer of the past with the similarly booted biker in his leathers today, or the woman flicking her glossy hair for the camera. People and their attitudes have not changed much and nor, when you think about it practically, have clothes: jackets, shirts, trousers, skirts, hats today all have to be designed to cover the same sort of bodies as they clothed a thousand years ago.

Setting a Social Structure

Dance and some non-naturalistic performance can be liberated from a social background. However, it is rare for any other sort of performance to exist without some sort of social class or power structure, and this structure needs to be made clear to the audience. In any play in which there is dialogue between characters it soon becomes obvious that they relate to each other in a way that demonstrates the differences in their background, age, intellect, strength, experience, and so on. The costume of the characters helps the audience to visualize the shifting graph of their power. This might sound complicated, as if the audience has to make intense, intellectual judgements with deliberate and frowning concentration throughout the play. But it's not like that. The designer has done all that deliberate and frowning concentration out of sight in her workroom in order to present the audience with a picture that they can assess with easy and practised familiarity.

Imagine a bus stop, and all the characters in any play you care to think of queuing for the bus. Perhaps, in this unlikely queue, you have Richard the Third, his brother the Duke of Clarence, their sister-in-law Anne, his sidekick Catesby and Clarence's murderers. Or perhaps it is Professor Higgins, Colonel Pickering, Eliza Doolittle, Eliza's father and Mrs Pearce waiting patiently for the *Pygmalion/My Fair Lady* bus. The audience should be able to gain, at a glance, a huge amount of information about the status of and relationship between the characters. They can only do that if the designer's research and work on the script has been thorough, and has been applied to the costumes.

Of course, there will be times when you want the audience to be unsure, when you want to befuddle or create the possibility of surprise. In such a case, the same amount of research and understanding will be used in a different way to confuse. The difference in the gamekeeper and the Duke who employs him may not be apparent in their clothes as they discuss the pheasants, and will only become apparent in their manner and speech.

*Class and power
structures can be
established within a
scene by the costume.*

Costume as Set

Budget, transport considerations when touring, the need to free as much stage space as possible for movement, or simply a preference for a minimalist style can result in the set being a space that is decorated and given life by the costumed actors. The costumes, and the lighting (which doubles in importance in such situations), can alter the perceptions of the audience with a fluidity and ease that is not always possible when the set has to be changed to reflect a change in situation. The costume designer is given a freedom to create a fast-changing world onstage using the moving bodies of the actors or dancers.

Imagine grandfather, mother, sisters, all in civilian clothes of 1914, waiting for news of their loved one, a young man who is away fighting in the war. The audience sees them in a pool of warm, indoor light. The light changes and takes the focus to the cold-lit battlefield where soldiers, in their muddy uniforms, fight for possession of the trench. The audience do not see the family, or, even if they do see them, the lack of light informs them to take no notice. They cannot see the trench or the enemy either, but the costume, light and sound enable their imagination to re-create a scene they have seen in news footage and films of the past. They will not all paint the same mental picture, but all members of the audience will believe it because they have created it for themselves – with the nudging help of the pictures they see onstage. It would be possible, having primed the audience's imagination in this way, to have a messenger onstage bringing the news from the battlefield to the drawing room through a lighting change. He would only need to remove his tin helmet and put down his rifle to be accepted as part of the civilian scene.

The whole stage can be dressed with colour and excitement by clothes. Actors do not always play people. They can be wind, trees, sea or desert. The audience will accept an actor as a storm or a horse, a concrete embodiment of grief or a chemical reaction – anything, in fact, provided it is presented in a way that signposts with clarity the way the genre needs to be understood. Some of the costume designer's most imaginative and creative work is involved with making these abstract possibilities into solid and practical fact.

Costume for Atmosphere

The combination of colour and light, particularly when combined with music, has the ability to change and create atmosphere. Everybody knows this and is affected by it all the time. It would be difficult to create a feeling of the gloom and threatening quality of a Dickensian den of thieves using bright, cheerful colours, or the rich opulence of an Arab court without the vibrant pattern and colour that we all associate with such a place. These are obvious examples but the same effect applies in situations that call for a more subtle realization. The flow and weight of cloth gives information about the weight of atmosphere – heaviness and thickness, diaphanous and airy, rich draping and folding, all conjure up related feelings in actors and audience.

COSTUME ON THE CAT-WALK

Cat-walk fashion in clothes is a strange and unreal thing. Look at a copy of *Vogue* or at models parading on the cat-walk and then imagine men and women actually walking around, having lunch, picking up children from school or attending a college lecture looking like those models. They would look as odd as creatures from another planet and the messages their clothes give out to the onlooker would tell nothing about their interior life and character, except to re-enforce their separation from the everyday life going on around them. The costume designer needs to look for inspiration not at the cat-walk but at the station platform or bus queue, where people are following their everyday routine, wearing what they usually wear. Costumes from the past can be equally confusing. Men and women dressed in their best

for their portrait. A picture of Lady What-Not in an art gallery may show her wandering round the garden but she will probably be dressed in a style that would be utterly impractical for any serious horticultural activity. A designer has to imagine the people living in the clothes, behaving as they would in the time, if she wants to create a convincing picture.

BALANCING INVENTION AND PRACTICALITY

Costume designing calls for a balanced mixture of invention and practicality – it is no good having one without the other. However brilliant your inventions, they are useless unless they can make the leap from the drawing of the picture in your head to practical, workable clothes that can be used onstage. It is equally useless to get trapped in the bog of the practical aspects of the production work, so that the creative leaps of invention become impossible. It works best when there is a good, firm base of research and preparation. The ground is prepared. The knowledge of the play and style and period are settled in and can be shoved to the back. All the ideas of character and colour hover around and there is a freedom to invent. And there is much more likelihood that the ideas will be appropriate and practical.

Talking about the ideas with other members of the production team is essential during the early stages of the design process. This means the designer has to be good at communicating ideas and thoughts with the group. The most difficult ideas to talk about are often the ones that seem either too vague to discuss or too impractical to achieve. It often happens that, when these ideas begin to be tossed about in discussion, they become clearer and more possible; the different perspectives and experiences of the members of the team can lead to new solutions to problems that seemed insurmountable. The best and most creative work is done when the director manages to assemble and mould a company of people who are confident enough of the support of the group to share all their ideas. Wonderful results have grown from ideas that seemed pretty shaky when they were first brought out in discussion. Others have been, probably quite rightly, dismissed in group discussions before money and time was wasted on them.

Costume design is not a job for someone who wants a starring role in a production. Everything you try to do with your designs is chosen to strengthen the performance of the actors and the concept of the director. Often, the costume designer's work is scarcely noticed by the audience – it can be so immersed in and natural to the actors' performances on stage that it seems to have arrived by accident. Costumes, however, are always noticed by the actors and play a huge part in the creation of the characters they play. There are times, of course, when you have the opportunity to create a stunning picture, or your skill is required to set a scene in a time or place, and your job is to make a visual atmosphere rather than help the characters get their message across to the audience. These opportunities are a playtime treat, and perhaps more akin to installation than costume design, as the audience reacts directly to the picture onstage rather than to the actor's interpretation.

Some of this sounds serious, technical and academic stuff. Of course, it is and can be. The reasons why fashion in clothes has been, and continues to be, influenced by politics, social change and economics is a fascinating study. But it is also a subject that that anyone who is interested can play with, enjoy and understand. The little girl dressing up as a bride in the bathroom net curtains shares the same interest as the social historian delving into rare texts in a university library and the teenager in the tattoo parlour; they are addressing the effect that outward appearance exerts on human beings. The theatre and costume designer or maker is lucky enough to play these games as a job. The research, the creation of the designs and the excitement of working with a team to put different worlds onstage, using such everyday stuff as clothes, make it a fascinating pursuit.

2 THE BEGINNING OF A PROJECT

The first sign of an exciting new project, even a sign as slight as a few words on the telephone, can send a crowd of visual ideas careering round your head. Tell your imagination to calm down, to wait a bit, and find out a few facts before it gets to work. There are a number of questions that must be answered before you surge away on the wrong track into a muddleheaded marsh.

EARLY QUESTIONS

Time

When is the first performance and how long is the rehearsal period?
Are you free to take the job, or does it interest you enough, creatively or financially, or both, to cram it in with other projects? Remember that it is extremely hard for performers and crew if the costume designer is not available during the technical and dress rehearsals, to answer questions or make or authorize alterations in design. No designer, however busy, grand and famous, has the right to complain about alterations to their stage pictures if they are not available to discuss possibilities.

If the dates of performance have not been set, and the project is to be realized through a series of workshops, it is helpful to know what the director or production manager hopes will happen. Devised work can have a much looser and more fragmented timescale for rehearsals. An idea may be worked on and experimented with for weeks or, occasionally, years. Actors, director and crew may

OPPOSITE: *Members of the company in Matthew Bourne's production of* Swan Lake. *Photo: Robbie Jack*

change and so may the designer. You should be aware, when working on a devised project, that your ideas belong to the project and may be taken over and developed by another designer later on in the process. No one in the freelance world can be sure of their plans a year ahead.

How much time will there be to research and design the costumes?
The depth of research required will depend on the project and on the designer's familiarity with the play and its place and period. It can take some time, for example, to ascertain the correct uniform and medals for an obscure soldier in an obscure war; in many cases, however, the non-naturalistic style of the play may allow you to invent a uniform that makes the audience feel they are seeing a Slavic cavalryman in a long-forgotten battle. It can also take time to assimilate the mood, story and relationships in a complicated script.

You have to decide yourself how long it will take you to create the designs once you have concluded the research. One set of designs may need to be built up over weeks, while another set may be blazed through in a matter of days. It is extremely difficult to hurry through designs, so try to leave as much time as possible; ideas are unreliable things and can sometimes clog up and rebel if rushed. And there is the familiar mental struggle when the urge for a new pencil, a different texture of paper, a cup of tea or a clean floor or, in fact, any distraction at all prevents you from sitting down and beginning to commit ideas to paper.

How much time will there be to shop for cloth and accessories and make the costumes or get the costumes made by others?
The length of rehearsal time is a good guide –

costumes cannot be cut until the play is cast and it will have to be cast by the first read-through. The length of time for the cutting and making depends of the number of people doing it and their experience and skill. Your designs should be practical within the limitations of your workforce.

How many performances are anticipated?
There is a difference in the way you make costumes for a show that is played for two or three performances and for one in which the clothes will be worn, washed and cleaned over a hundred or more nights. On a show that will have only a single performance, remember that costumes will still have to be strong enough to cope with the technical and dress rehearsal.

Budget
The budget will play a significant part in dictating how the costumes will be realized.

How much is the costume budget?
Costume budgets vary enormously from project to project. If you accept a job, you accept any restrictions of budget as well. It is no good having the most wonderful ideas if there is not enough money to make them come true, and the audience never sees them. You have to train your imagination to behave itself and be reasonable – but not too reasonable, and certainly not down-trodden. You must also train it to be brave and not give in too easily. The unaffordable pictures in your head may be adapted to give the audience an equally vivid experience for less money. Expensive costumes are not necessarily better and good ideas are worth far more to the audience than real leather or pure silk. And, if there is really no substitute for a special effect than leather or silk, a way may be found by budget-juggling and careful shopping on other items so that you can buy some of what you want.

How will expenses be reclaimed?
Most companies are trustworthy and will either give you a float of money for shopping, or reimburse you promptly on production of receipts. If you feel any nagging doubts, do not spend your own money until you have discussed the system in place for reclaiming it with the production manager, society treasurer, or whoever is controlling the company money. Reclaim money frequently until you are sure the system works or ask for a petty-cash float in advance. Be suspicious if there is a suggestion that you will be paid back once box-office money comes in; there is a possibility it may never arrive.

There can be a problem in getting receipts when shopping in markets or car-boot or rummage sales. Keep a list, with dates and places, of anything you buy and warn the money-manager of the company that receipts may not be available for some items. Of course, if you are rich enough not to worry, or you feel it is worth the risk because you love the project so much, none of this applies. But at least you will be forewarned. Many of the most exciting projects are created on a shoestring.

Does the company have any special arrangements with suppliers?
Some companies have accounts with local shops or theatrical suppliers. The production manager will provide information and requisition forms where necessary and there will probably be a catalogue of the goods they supply somewhere in the theatre. Local companies may offer special rates in exchange for free advertising in the programme, in which case the information must be passed on to whoever is responsible for the content of the programme as soon as possible. Programme information will have to be with the printers some time before the first night and people can get pretty cross if their promised credit or free advertisement for a service fails to materialize.

Does the company own a stock of costumes?
Many theatre companies have a store of costumes and accessories and these can save the budget a chunk of money. It is well worth spending a day rooting through this store before you start buying, in case there is anything that can be incorporated into the production you are designing.

What is the running budget for the show?
Costumes need washing, cleaning and repairing

and it can be forgotten by the company that the costume designer's contract and contact with the production may well end on the first night. It is helpful if the designer and maker are aware at the start of the design process of the sort of support that will be available during the run for the care of the costumes, so that they may choose cloth that will be appropriate. Dry cleaning is expensive, ironing can be a lengthy process and the company may not have budgeted for a Wardrobe Master or Mistress to look after this aspect of the production. Three or four hours a day can be saved if washing, drying, ironing, and the sort of wear the costume will have to put up with, have been taken into account in the early stages of design. Costumes should look as good on the last night as on the first and some of the responsibility for this rests with the designer and shopper.

The Venue

The venue plays a strong part in deciding the style of your design. It dictates how the audience will see your costumes, and you have to keep the distance of the audience from the stage in mind. Details that look interesting in the fitting room may vanish when viewed from further away.

Is it a traditional theatre space?
In the more traditional venues the audience will be seeing your costumes from differing viewpoints. The front row of the stalls may be just two or three metres (6–10ft) from the nearest actor, while the back row of the gallery may be as much as or more than fifty metres (55yds) away. You have to design clothes that look unexaggerated to the eyes of the nearest people, but are at the same time capable of carrying their messages to those who are much further away.

Is it close work?
A studio production, a play in the round or on a thrust stage, or a promenade performance will bring the audience close, and in some cases to within touching or smelling distance of the actors. That useful and consoling phrase 'it will look all right under the lights' will cease to be either true or consoling, and the detail and cleanliness of

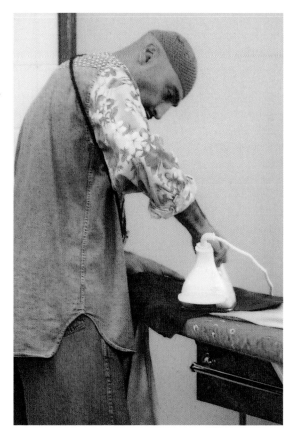

Pressing costumes in the wardrobe before the performance. Photo: Charlotte Cunningham

costumes becomes much more urgent. Lights and distance can make a grubby, grey, make-up-smeared collar appear to be fresh from the laundry, but close viewing, or an open-air performance in daylight, will show it up in the true light of reality. In this sort of situation, clumsy fastenings, dirty shoes and threadbare ties can only pass muster when they would, in reality, be worn by the character.

Is it long-distance work?
There are times when the costumes have to look good from a distance but will never be seen close up. A carnival or pageant will show the characters as a group and the general impression of colour, shape and richness will become much more

important than the detail. Time is wasted on careful work that will be visible only to other performers, although it is easy to forget this when you are working on the costumes and your eyes are so close to the work. Stand back and look. Half-close your eyes to test the impression of the sights the far-off audience will see.

EARLY DISCUSSIONS

The first thing you will want to know is what the play is about. There may not be a script but there will be an idea. Early discussion with the director will establish the story, the style and the period. The story may still be vague, but the style – naturalistic, abstract, fairy tale, melodramatic, or whatever – will exist in the director's mind. This information will help nudge your imagination in the most useful direction before you begin the research work and risk wasting time on ideas that are inappropriate to the genre.

It can happen that the way you see the work developing differs radically from the vision in the director's mind. Disagreements of this kind can lead to an exciting new approach, particularly when the director/designer partnership has been

well tried and tested through past experience. If, however, you cannot understand and visualize the director's point of view, it might be better to re-consider accepting the job. In practice, this insurmountable barrier rarely occurs unless the director has no input at all into the choice of designer.

The First Reading

The first reading of the script is, to many designers, a key to the whole design process of the project. As such, it is worth being prepared to catch any ideas at their conception. Most designers have some sort of ritual for this moment. It may be the cup-of-tea-and-feet-on-the-kitchen-table approach, the clear-desk-sharp-pencil-aligned-notebook, or the corner-table-in-a-café; experience will tell you which method makes you most receptive to the pictures that leap out of the script into your mind.

A number of useful preparations can be made before the first reading. Make sure you have the sort of clothes worn by the people at the time of the play fixed in your head. Flick through a period costume book to remind yourself of the shape of hat, of skirts, of trousers, and the posture of the people at the time of the play you are about to read.

The detail of these street procession costumes is highlighted with white.

This is not thorough research. It is a reminder to make sure your mind will show you useful pictures.

The ideas, emotions and visual pictures that arise from this first reading of the script may be the most valuable of the whole design process; be sure to note them down, as they may become obscured later by more precise study, and muddled by research. This encounter with the story is the closest you will ever get to seeing the work in the same way as the audience does. They see it once, and all their reactions to the performance will be immediate and uncluttered by analysis. Yours, as you read and re-read the script, research its background and period, discuss the process in production meetings and watch the actors in rehearsal, will alter as your familiarity with the work develops.

Hold on tight to those first, fresh pictures; you may need to return to them later if your ideas become muddy, stale or over-complicated by a knowledge that the audience do not possess. It is easy to forget you are designing for them and not for fellow members of your profession.

Script Analysis

The world the characters live in will be apparent in the script, although it may be buried deep. It is a world of atmosphere as much as it is one of political, historical and social fact, and this atmosphere may be elusive. The first page of *The Cherry Orchard* presents an immediate and clear picture of the naturalistic world its characters inhabit; the prologue to Shakespeare's *Henry V* tells us that we must imagine a particular world at war. A play such as Sarah Kane's *4.48 Psychosis* or Lorca's *Blood Wedding* hides its world from us at the start and reveals it slowly through successive scenes. Before you can start designing the costumes you need to dig out the secrets of their background.

The study of the characters depends not only on their nature but also on their relative power and their importance to each other. This is not the same as their importance to the story. It makes no difference to the design of the costume if the character appears onstage for one minute or plays a major part in every scene. The picture created in that single minute may remain for fifty years in the mind of the audience member who sees it. No one could forget the messenger who appears once in Euripides' play *Hippolytus*, bringing Theseus the news of the terrible death of his son; The Prince of Verona, who appears onstage for a few moments during Romeo and Juliet's love story, leaves the audience with their final picture of their sad, grand world.

The 'power chart' that you make maps the relationship and relative strengths and social positions of the characters in the play. It may be influenced by class, rank, political power, family relationships, or many other factors, and it will affect the way costumes relate to each other within scenes. It helps the audience to engage with the plot if they can see who is the servant and who is the master, which is powerful sister and which is the weaker. It makes the occasions when you want the audience to be unsure more likely to succeed. Peter Pan is a 'lost boy'. But if he looks exactly the same as the other 'lost boys', are you transferring the message you want to the audience?

The Costume Plot

Before you begin work on the costumes, you will need to have made a costume plot. This is a chart that will tell you at a glance which characters appear in each scene, what costumes and accessories you must design, and when the costume changes occur. Alterations to the scripted information, which will happen in rehearsal, can be marked in as the work proceeds. This chart, if kept up to date, will help to make sure designer and maker know every costume item that will be used in the performance. Checking through it with actors at fittings will bring to light any information that has not reached the Wardrobe via the stage manager or director.

The basis of the costume plot will come directly from the script, but some of the information you need will be hidden. Many writers do not mention costume in their script and all the information will have to be gathered from the dialogue and the action.

Example

This is an extract from the beginning of *A Doll's House* by Henrik Ibsen. The play was written in 1879 and takes place in the Helmers' house. The stage directions describe a sitting room and tell us that it is winter.

(A bell rings in the hall; shortly afterwards the door is heard to open. Enter NORA, humming a tune and in high spirits. She is in out-door dress and carries a number of parcels; these she lays on the table to the right. She leaves the outer door open after her, and through it is seen a PORTER who is carrying a Christmas tree and a basket, which he gives to the MAID who has opened the door.)
NORA. Hide the Christmas Tree carefully, Helen. Be sure the children do not see it till this evening, when it is dressed. (To the PORTER, taking out her purse.) How much?
PORTER. Sixpence.
NORA. Here is a shilling. No, keep the change. (The PORTER thanks her and goes out. NORA shuts the door. She is laughing to herself, as she takes off her hat and coat. She takes a packet of macaroons from her pocket and eats one or two; then goes cautiously to her husband's room and listens.) Yes, he is in. (Still humming, she goes to the table on the right.)
HELMER. *(Calls out from his room.)* Is that my little lark twittering out there?

The action at the beginning of the play gives several facts which are relevant to costume:

- Nora comes in from outside in a hat and coat, which she takes off on stage.
- The coat needs a pocket with an opening wide enough for her to extricate the bag of macaroons that she is eating onstage. Check with stage manager the size of the bag so that it will fit in the pocket.
- The porter is carrying a basket. Will the Wardrobe or props department provide the basket?
- Nora gives the porter money from her purse. Helmer gives her some money later in the scene after she has taken off her coat. She will presumably put it in the same purse. Does she need a pocket in her dress for this purse and how big will it be?
- Although there is no mention in the stage directions of her gloves, our knowledge of the etiquette of the period informs us that she would also have been wearing gloves and anyway it is Christmas and winters in Norway are cold and snowy.

All this information is gleaned from a few lines of script and needs to be written into the costume plot. A costume plot for some of the characters who appear in *A Doll's House* might look like the following:

Name	Act I – daytime	Act II – late afternoon the next day	Act III – the following evening
Nora	Day dress with pocket, coat with pocket, hat, gloves, purse	Dress, cloak, hat. In box – fancy dress, muff, gloves, flesh-coloured stockings and shawl all as worn in Act III. Hair falls down onstage.	Fancy-dress costume as seen in Act II. Quick change (2 mins?) to day dress. Cloak, hat, bag, ring.
Porter	Outdoor clothes, basket.		
Maid	Indoor dress	Indoor dress	'Half-dressed.' (Night clothes?)
Helmer	Indoor clothes, purse in pocket, coat and hat.	Coat, hat and suit.	Evening dress, Domino (which is a cloak), pocket for keys.

RESEARCH

The research you do before and during the designing of the costumes varies in content and detail according to the project and its genre. A naturalistic play that is to be performed in a naturalistic style will give you a clear lead to the sort of research you need. The mainstay of your sources will be art galleries and reproductions of paintings, contemporary photographs if the play takes place after the invention of the camera, costume collections and museums. Costumes are always influenced by the period in which they are created; you have only to compare the hairstyles and make-up of a 'Tudor' heroine filmed in the 1920s, 1950s and 1980s to see how much design reflects the idea of beauty fashionable in those eras. And we can't be smug about it, because it's an odds-on bet that our ideas will look just as dated thirty years from today.

You have to be selective and quite suspicious when you are researching the past. Future researchers could look at photographs of people today at the State Opening of the Houses of Parliament, or at a convention of Hell's Angels, and imagine that those people were wearing the standard dress of the time. The more you read about the lives and manners of our ancestors, the more able you will be to transform the smartened-up versions on the gallery walls to a more gritty reality in your designs.

Do not be misled into believing that your most painstaking research will result in a true re-creation of the past. We live in a different world. Our eyes, noses, ears and preconceptions are not the same as those of people living even fifty years ago, let alone two or three hundred years. The most faithful and accurate pictures will be looked at by an audience that belongs to the twenty-first century. Everything you put on stage is for them, to help them to imagine and relate to the lives of the characters. This means that the research you do into the hearts, souls and daily life of the people in the script is every bit as important as, and perhaps

LEFT TO RIGHT: **An unknown girl in the eighteenth century (Photo: Mike Murnane), The Right Honourable Chichester S.P. Fortescue in the nineteenth century (Photo: Mike Murnane) and Angela O'Brian McDonnell in the twentieth century all send us messages about the clothes and the attitudes of their eras.**

more important than, your research into period costume.

There will always be someone in the auditorium who knows more about some detail of period or formal costume than you do. But the bulk of the audience will see the overall effect and will not be worried by two points instead of one on the linen handkerchief in the jacket breast pocket, or share Beau Brummel's obsession with the folds of a cravat. They will not recognize that the leading man's jacket is crumpled because it is made of pure Irish linen; they will see a jacket that appears to have been pulled, crumpled, from a heap on the floor, and will get a picture of an uncared-for appearance rather than of fashionable elegance.

Paintings of the Past

People tended to be painted in their best clothes and the painter may also have been paid to flatter his subjects. The clothes in historical portraits have as much relation to the clothes of the day as the fashions of the cat-walk have to what people are wearing in today's queue at the supermarket check-out. Portraits, particularly those that were painted before the twentieth century, do provide many clues as to the way clothes were made and worn. But very few people would have had the means at their disposal to pay for cloth and braid, a tailor and a wig maker, and would have lived the sort of life that made these clothes practical. Try translating the clothes of the past into a present-day version – perhaps the Savile Row suit, the hand-made shirt and the silk designer shirt; the sword replaced by the most up-to-the-minute mobile phone and palm top; the wig by the all-year tan and a fashionable hairstyle. How often, when not in the office, would the gym-toned body be seen in T-shirt and shorts, in a towelling bath-robe, in casual jacket and jeans? The same must have been true in the past and it is the job of the costume designer to create a similar richness of style in period costume.

Cartoons and Sketches

Cartoons are particularly useful as they tend to use idiosyncratic costume to demonstrate the character of their subject in the same way as a designer of pantomime or expressionist costume might – employing a degree of exaggeration or simplification of style to make a point. The sketch books of many artists, even those who specialize in formal portraits, often contain lively information about the ordinary people dressed in everyday clothes going about their work.

Costume Collections

There are many excellent, specialist costume collections and most local museums have a few costumes on display. Here you can see the real thing, study the cut of the clothes and see how the cloth hangs. The collection may have items that are not on show and it is always possible to arrange to see these hidden treasures, although the larger museums may ask you to make an appointment weeks in advance. It is surprising how often undiscovered antique clothes turn up in jumble or car-boot sales. They may be in a sad state of repair but they can still make the costume researcher's heart beat faster; they offer the opportunity to handle the cloth, to peer at the way the seams have been stitched, and imagine the person from the past who wore it.

Films

Be wary of films made after the time you are researching even if the subject is appropriate; the clothes in these films have been created by a designer, and you have no true idea of their accuracy. Documentaries and newsreels, however, are an excellent source and can show a wide spectrum of society in everyday clothes. Advertisements from the past provide an interesting subject; they show a contemporary, but idealized view of life. Advertisers use their knowledge of the way we would like to live or look or be seen, and, in doing so, tell us a great deal about the social aspirations of people of the past.

Photographs

Collections of photographs in photo libraries or books give a wonderful, varied and accurate picture of the more recent past and the oldest photographs give us some of the clearest images of the later Victorians. The texture of the clothes, the

Advertisements show an idealized picture of fashion in the 1950s.

thickness of binding, the buttonholes and signs of wear show us a less elegant and more believable picture of those much-idealized men and women. Old newspapers and journals have illustrations taken directly from life.

Reminiscence

Talking to the people who wore the clothes can be the best research and their memories will be jogged by your interest. It is as much of a pleasure for most elderly people to delve back into their memories as it is a pleasure for the researcher to hear first-hand descriptions of the fashions of other times. A stocking, a stiff collar, a photograph or an advertisement will almost certainly unlock a headful of memories, particularly in women. People tend to keep a clear picture of the clothes they wore in their youth and, if you ask them to describe their teenage party dress or the school clothes of their childhood, their recall may be very clear, even when later memories have faded.

The Internet

The Internet gives you access to material from libraries and collections all over the world and to huge amounts of costume information. The difficulty lies in sorting the good stuff from the useless junk, and this can present an almost insurmountable problem for novice costume researcher. Until you have a good base of knowledge yourself, you cannot tell if the material you are finding comes from a reliable source or has been produced by someone with even less knowledge and experience than yourself. Once you have a clear picture of what you are looking for, and can distinguish opinion from fact, you can narrow down the search and gain access to a wonderful variety of information. Be prepared for some unusual discoveries, too, as costume attracts the fetishists as well as the designers.

Novels and Biographies

Words from the past can paint a clear picture for us today, a picture that is adapted by our modern brains into a message that can be understood and de-coded by today's audience. It is an interesting exercise to draw a character in costume from a description in a novel of the time. This extract from Charlotte Bronte's *Jane Eyre* describes the uniform of some charity-school girls in the mid-nineteenth century:

> The eighty girls sat motionless and erect: a quaint assemblage they appeared, all with plain locks combed from their faces, not a curl visible; in brown dresses, made high and surrounded by a narrow tucker around the throat, with little pockets of Holland (shaped something like a Highlander's purse) tied in front of their frocks, and designed to serve the purpose of a workbag: all too wearing woollen stockings and country made shoes, fastened with brass buckles.

Working Clothes

It is difficult to research working clothes, particularly those from pre-camera days. It used to be an expensive and lengthy business to make a visual record of people and events. Portraits were commissioned by the prosperous, and usually show people in their best clothes. If a portrait was commissioned of servants, their working clothes would be cleaned up for the occasion, to demonstrate the prosperity and taste of their master or mistress. Clothes lasted a long time in the past. A dress might be altered, mended and dyed, or even completely re-made, with the cloth inside-out to show the unworn side. When it had gone through all these stages the garment might be handed on to the lady's maid, who in turn altered, mended, dyed and turned it. Even after that, the dress might be cut down for a child, and by the time it reached the very poor, perhaps as a charitable gift, it would be in a very sad state.

The clothes of the poor and the workers are often recorded in words, as in the extract from *Jane Eyre* above, and these words, after some preparatory research into the period, can be translated by us into pictures. The first thing to do is to check when the story was written and make sure you have the right idea in your head of an assortment of clothes of the time. Then begin to draw, using your knowledge of the character in the story to pad out the description on the page. Not only will the clothes have a reality that may not exist in a formal

*Checking the detail
of a naturalistic
uniform.*

portrait, but also your understanding of the way the character wears them, and the sort of clothes they would like or dislike, will give a particular life to the costume.

Looking at Life

We are surrounded by the clothes of our own time and, when you look out for it, by the clothes of the last forty years. It is a mistake to think that the style of clothes changes quickly. There may be yearly upheavals amongst young people in the fashionable world but many clothes worn by ordinary people today could, with some slight adjustments of length and accessories, have been worn thirty or forty years ago. The costume designer dresses characters who must appear to belong to many different ages, professions and classes, and the best way to research a contemporary play is to look at contemporary people in the same situation. The clothes worn by shoppers in a designer boutique in the city will not be the same as the clothes worn by those searching for bargains in a country market. If you have to dress lawyers, hang about outside law courts; if it is schoolteachers you need, watch the gates at the end of the school day. The audience are much more likely to notice any mistakes in modern clothes

than they are in a costume drama, so it's important to get it right.

The main figure or group in a portrait or the detail in a landscape is sometimes supported by subsidiary figures, and the carter loading up his hay-wain in the background or the fisherman checking lobster pots at the edge of a seascape can give us clues about working costume. Some painters from the past, such as Hogarth and George Morland, did paint scenes of working life. But often the most valuable resource is cartoon and book illustration. The drawings of Phiz, who illustrated for Charles Dickens, show a vivid, lively and un-romanticized version of Victorian life; perhaps the comic nature of the illustration cuts through the sentiment and varnish of the era and shows us a flash of the true life of the past.

Uniforms

The work of reproducing accurate uniforms is expensive and difficult. Perhaps 'expensive *or* difficult' would be a better way of putting it. If you can afford to hire the costume from a firm that specializes in military costumes and other uniforms, their expertise, stock, buttons and medals will be at your disposal. But if you are working on a tighter budget, and have to research for yourself without expert help, it is wise to be wary of attempting a naturalistic accuracy and to opt instead for a representation of the uniform rather than an accurate re-construction.

A straight choice, decreed by the budget, may force you to choose between hiring an accurate costume and creating a version of the uniform that will be recognized and accepted by most of the audience. Take, for example, a traditional British policeman. The uniform and accessories are complicated and precise, and change every few years, but the image most people have in their heads remains the same: the dark, navy uniform with silver buttons, and the bell-shaped hat, whistle, belt and truncheon. An expert could date a correct costume to within a few years but the average member of the audience will not recall exact details of buttons and tabs.

PRODUCTION MEETINGS

All the departments working on a project use production meetings to pool ideas and report and share progress, but the primary importance of such meetings is to make sure that everyone understands the way the director has interpreted the script, and that everyone is working towards the same goal. If you have worked with the director before, you will share points of reference from past jobs and the nature of the work will become clear in the first moments of the meeting. With a new colleague, it always helps if you can do some research into their past work before starting discussions so that you have some points of reference in common. Try to find as much time as you need to talk together and share ideas, and make certain that you understand each other well.

Ascertaining Style and Genre

Every member of the production team creates its jigsaw pieces of the production in different ways. The whole jumble of ideas is put together in the final stages of production. The pieces must blend into one and the joints between the pieces must be invisible. For this seamless blending to occur, the style of the piece must be clear and precise before the designs are begun. This style, sometimes

referred to as 'genre', depends as much on the director as on the script.

Imagine you are working on a dance piece. It could be performed in the tutus and tights and ballet shoes that have long been the standard style of costume for classical ballet. It could be a newly choreographed piece, with barefoot men and women appearing nearly naked onstage. It could be a reflection on modern society, with the dancers appearing to be wearing the ordinary clothes of today. The sets and lighting on the stage where these pieces are performed will reflect the genre as much as the costumes: the nymphs in their tutus dance in dappled light through a romantic forest; the barefoot, naked company, lit by harsh side-lighting, move in a minimalist monochrome world; the familiar high street of the third group is suggested by the bus stops, road signs and neon billboards of modern, urban life. These simple, unsubtle examples show how essential it is that designers and performers are sure of the style that they will be helping to create.

Suitability of Design for the Project

A number of other factors influence the style of design. You may be working on a production with forty children, with inexperienced helpers and very little money and time. In such a case, the only way to turn them into characters in a jungle story may be to forget complicated costumes and concentrate on creating patterns for masks and tails which can be made by the children themselves or their parents. The simplicity and home-made look of the costumes, particularly if worn with a carefully chosen basic costume which uses clothes the children already possess, will make a virtue out of necessity.

At the opposite end of the scale, you may find yourself with three actors and enough money to pay for anything that comes into your head. This should makes things easy, but it will throw up different problems; more people will be employed to create the costumes you have designed, and it will become vital for you to check every detail as your costumes are constructed by makers.

In the first case, you will probably become closely involved with all the actors and makers; in the second, it will be more usual to meet the actors only at fittings, and your input into the realization of the design and the way it works with the body of the actor may be minimal.

Discovering the Concept

It is possible to interpret a script in many different ways. Fashion, budget, politics, personal interest, funding, experience and company style can all influence the way a director envisages the performance. It is likely, if the work is popular, that many of the company will have worked on another production of the same piece. In this case, they will all need to forget what they did last time and approach the work from a fresh angle that supports the work of the present company.

Shakespeare's *Hamlet* is a good example. An experienced costume designer may have worked on the play three or four times. Perhaps the first director set it in a Jacobean court, the second up-dated it to the 1960s, the third devised a movement piece round the interpretation of Hamlet's confusion and Ophelia's madness, and the fourth used puppets for the Ghost and the Players and a filmed sequence to accompany Gertrude's description of Ophelia's death. By the time a designer has worked on these four productions, he or she knows the play very well indeed, may have watched it being performed, in rehearsals as well as in performance, twenty or thirty times, and could probably work as a prompter without a copy of the script for any scene that includes a costume change.

Of course, it is useful to have such an intimate knowledge of the characters and their relationships, and to be forewarned about problem costumes, such as that of the ghost of Hamlet's father. However, the director's vision of the current production will be new and different and the costume designs must spring from a fresh reading of the text by the designer, with the new concept to the fore and the old ones forgotten.

Communication

It takes practice to communicate ideas in a meeting, and concentration, imagination and openness to absorb the ideas of others. Listening is as great a skill as talking. It can be daunting to try to explain your ideas to a group of directors, other designers, production managers and stage managers whom you have never met before, particularly if, as is the case with many designers, communication is easier with pen and paper than with words. It is essential to be well prepared, having done a certain amount of research and developed a familiarity with the script or information about the project. This background knowledge will help you understand what other people are talking about, as well as giving you the confidence to present your own ideas clearly. In this way, the ground will be well prepared for the new ideas that will spring from this first meeting with the team.

First Meetings

Matters of fees and budgets will be discussed privately, but it is best if the early production meetings combine as many of the production team as can be assembled at this early stage. It can be easier for the costume designer to talk about ideas and plans alone with the director but the advantage of discussing ideas with a larger group very quickly becomes obvious. It is easy to become hooked on an idea or a style that does not gel with the overall production. It is a simple matter to recognize and overcome misconceptions at an early stage of the design process, but much harder to adjust once an idea has become embedded into the designs. The process of opening up your vision of the play to a larger group encourages you to view the picture in your mind from a new angle and test the way your ideas look to an outside eye. Other members of the team will benefit in the same way from this general scrutiny. New ideas will emerge, and old ideas will be refined in the melting pot.

It can be difficult not to feel protective about your own ideas and to feel defensive when they do not ring bells in the imagination of others. It can be equally difficult to open your own mind to ideas that are opposed to your own. The trick is to imagine yourself as the audience and remember that they are the people who matter most. It is also salutary to remember that experience, so often

jaques at school.   Older Jaques   vest & bare feet Jaques.

Jaques at home.   passenger   Jean.   Driver.

Rough sketches of costumes present an idea of the style of the finished production.

used as a tool for predicting grim disaster, is not always the best tool for inventing the new. A young, fresh mind can produce a sparkling idea that can be helped to practical fruition by more experienced members of the team. Remember that ideas belong to the project and do not remain in your own keeping.

It is always useful to make rough sketches of your ideas, even if you draw as you talk. It is counter-productive, however, if these are too finished as this will make it less easy for others to feel that they can make alternative suggestions.

Secondary Meetings

These meetings will involve presentation and discussion of designs. The designer should present small sketches of characters in costume in a group scene, or sketches that show the progression of a character in costume through the play, so that there is something tangible to discuss. Any tricky decisions involving costume should be addressed. Quick changes may need action within a scene or the addition of some lines to the script to allow the actor enough time. Questions about doubling (when one actor plays two or more characters) must be resolved, as must any confusion over which props will be designed by the costume designer and which by the set designer.

The age of the characters may need to be set; after all, a grandmother could be in her early thirties or her late seventies. Are Macbeth's witches Gothic lasses or aged crones? Make sure you know the director's thoughts on all the characters and make your own thoughts clear, to avoid having to re-work designs at a later stage.

The designer should use the early meetings to gain a certain understanding of the genre of the production so that it can be reflected in the feeling and style of the costume designs. Production meetings will continue to happen right up to the final dress rehearsal and will be called whenever it becomes necessary to share and pool information between members of the team. In addition, there may be a need for a production meeting when some urgent problem surfaces during the technical and dress rehearsals of production week.

Later Meetings

The set designer and costume designer will have exchanged ideas about colours and lighting and, by the time the final series of production meetings start to happen, the costume designs will have been completed. The search for samples of cloth and haberdashery will have begun and decisions will have been made about wigs and footwear. Changes will still be made to the designs, and some questions, particularly those that relate to casting, will remain unanswered. The inspiration for the costume may change when you find out that a beer-bellied giant of an actor has been cast as the skinny spindleshanks of your imagination; or that the colours of set and costumes will not look good together in a particular scene. The portfolio of designs can be spread out at a meeting and looked at in conjunction with the set designs to create a picture of the play.

The more you can get right at this stage, the better. Once the costumes have been bought, cut or made, any changes become expensive and time-consuming. It may take only an hour to alter the design, but it can take many hours to re-cut and re-make a costume.

Emergency Meetings

These worrying meetings tend to happen, if they happen at all, close to opening night. There are all sorts of reasons for them, from a last-minute cast change or a financial crisis with the management to, most worrying for the costume department, a costume that simply does not work. It may look wrong onstage; perhaps it reacts in the wrong way to the lights; may be the director hates it or the actor is unable to work in it. Such things happen, and they almost always happen when the workload is at its heaviest and nerves are strained. A solution will be found if everyone sticks closely to the facts and remembers that the meeting has been arranged to solve a problem and not to allot responsibility or blame. The difficult part is deciding what to do and accepting that it needs to be done. Once that has been achieved, the actual work involved, which may have seemed impossible, becomes manageable with the help of the team.

3 CREATING THE DESIGNS

DEFINING THE STYLE

The way costumes will be designed and made will be influenced by the budget, the timescale, the venue and the experience of the company and its audience. These, and many other, factors have as significant a place in deciding the style of the designs as the actual content of the project. The suggestions in this chapter give a guide to some different styles. Of course, they overlap, and nothing in the world onstage is as clear-cut as it appears when filed neatly under academic headings. These suggestions are very rough divisions which waver and blur in reality.

Naturalistic

A naturalistic style of costume aims to make people look as they would if they were living an everyday life at the time and in the place the performance is set. In reality, the clothes are as much of an illusion as any other kind of stage costume. Designers who have tried to make genuine historical copies of costumes of the past have run into difficulties when the actors, with their modern bodies and attitudes, try to work in accurate reproductions of period clothes. Edwardian ladies did not have broad shoulders and gym-toned muscles. They never learnt to run or stride. The movement classes of a modern actress's training encourage her to move with freedom and relaxation; her body is not trained to cope with the arduous restrictions that would have dogged the Edwardian young lady from childhood, from the

OPPOSITE: **The Beau Defeated,** *by Mary Pix. Director Nicky Ramsay, designer Tina Bicât, for St Mary's College.* Photo: Robin Cottrell

time when she was first encased in corset bones from chin to thigh. Indeed, the modern body is certain to rebel against such restriction. Think of the contrast between a childhood free-bodied in Lycra and cotton jersey and trainers, and a childhood swathed in calf-length layers of wool and starched cotton, and stiff-buttoned boots.

A different effect occurs with modern-dress productions. It may seem, in a production about (for instance) a building site, that the actors could be dressed in the same clothes that you would see on a real building site. But, once again, it doesn't work if reality is put onstage. There will be problems with the characters looking too much alike, in their yellow safety waistcoats and hats, and the audience will have trouble sorting out who is who. The hats may create shadows that hide the actors' eyes. The clothes, which might look worn and dirty in the light of day, suddenly look clean and over-smart in the stage lighting and have to be

Art and Practicality

Costumes, both in their design and their construction, must be practical. Designers and makers can never, even in their most imaginative dreams, forget that the picture they are creating will be worn by active, hard-working humans. The starched high cravat, which appears so tight and unyielding, must allow the actor space to swell his throat when singing; the corset, which seems so tight-laced to the audience, must allow for the rib expansion an actress needs to produce enough vocal power to send a whisper to the back row of the gallery.

painted and broken down to look anything like work clothes. A stage can become overloaded with one colour or texture and the overall picture will be dull and uninformative.

The skill of design comes in pulling out the essence of the period and people; of using the messages (such as the hard hat, the corseted silhouette) to suggest the period and place to the audience and give pictures on the stage that will clarify the characters and their world. Never under-estimate the audience. They may look at the pictures you put on stage with a modern and unprofessional eye, but they are wonderfully adept at de-coding the messages you put into the costumes. It is only fair that the messages have been composed for today's everyman and woman to understand and not for people who have studied historical and stage costume.

Exaggerated Costume

Some projects demand a style of costume that is an exaggeration of reality, or plays with the theatricality of the performance. The more

traditional musicals can provide obvious examples. The famous Ascot scene for the film of *My Fair Lady*, designed by Cecil Beaton, shows us a cross-section of upper-class English men and women who all dress in the height of Edwardian fashion – but in black and white. Exaggerated silhouettes, larger-than-life hats, over-large patterned fabrics and an excessive range of colour and sparkle take this style of design away from any sort of reality that you might find in the street.

Masks, and heavy stylized make-up, have been used for thousands of years to clarify and simplify the message to the audience. It could seem as if a masked actor could only display one emotion, but a good mask, when worn by an actor who can use it well, can send a powerful and varied range of feeling to the audience. Costume for masked productions needs to be simple, as the attention must be drawn to the face and body of the actor, and not distracted by complications of cloth. Places where the mask meets the costume, such as the edge of the face, the neck and the shoulders, must be considered carefully; an awkward

LEFT AND OPPOSITE:
Exaggerations in design have a place in both comic and serious performance.

MRs SINBAD
"Shipwrecked"

Palm
leaf hair.

'Leaves'
painted on
cloth.

Poss with
green ist enha...
skirt underneal...

conjuncture, or a difference in style, makes it harder for the audience to believe in the mask. The costume needs to be designed to suit the mask, and as a continuation of the spirit of the mask, rather than as a separate dress.

Productions for an audience of children often make use of a simplified or exaggerated version of reality. This works when the subject demands a storybook style, and small children do enjoy bright colours and sparkle, but it can become the visual equivalent of talking down to children. In fact, younger people are as good as adults at interpreting the messages given by costume.

Pantomime is at one end of this scale and the abstract surrealism of expressionist theatre at the other. Both turn the characters inside-out so that their lives, thoughts and emotional states are displayed with an easily understood clarity to the audience.

Some countries have a tradition of using puppetry to present political and highly emotive themes, and their audiences are used to interpreting the exaggerations of costume. Many companies in Britain, particularly those using devising and a director/designer partnership to create plays, find a freedom of expression in an exaggerated and non-naturalistic design concept, and their work has accustomed theatre audiences to accepting this exciting development. It becomes particularly important, when working in this style that the script, music, lighting, sound, style of acting and costume and set design are closely linked, and the design team may well work with the company throughout much of the rehearsal period to build the design concept along with the performances. Not that this style of costuming performers is new – dance, circus, mummers, vaudeville, music hall have used it for years. But surrealistic, exaggerated and abstract costume in serious drama is relatively new to many British theatregoers today and, because it is rarely used on film or television for adults, it still packs a good, strong punch.

Costume for Devised Theatre

The design work for devised performance becomes looser, more adaptable and less rigid than that for a scripted play. You cannot know before the beginning of rehearsal how the work is going to proceed and how it will look. You may have an idea of the style, the period and the number of performers, and you will have some idea of the subject matter. However, the detail, the characterization of the roles, the movement, and the emotional journey of the story and its participants will all be created through rehearsal. The whole basis of a devised piece is that it is invented through experiment by the company and crew, and the designer needs to be in rehearsal watching the process.

Devised work forges strong director/designer partnerships. When this relationship has been tried and tested through several productions, it will become impossible to tell where ideas originate and who began a train of thought. A designer in rehearsal can inspire the imagination of the actors by building on and facilitating the work they do. At the same time, the designer must make sure that the final picture the audience sees does not become fragmented and overcomplicated by the bubbling invention that will spring from rehearsal. The most important task may involve paring down, ordering and clarifying the ideas.

Signs and Symbols

Imagine a black box of a stage with a single spotlight. Into the spotlight comes an actor all in black. Put a crown on him and he is a King. Put a ragged hood on him and he is a beggar. Give him a skirt and he is a woman. Give him a mane and a tail and he is a lion. Give him the mask of grief and he is grief. The audience, when the actor is good at his job, and the picture they see is presented with movement and confidence, will accept the limitations of the style and fill in the gaps for themselves. The addition of sound – the fanfare, the waltz, the roar – will make the picture even clearer. These representations of character and status are symbols and signs that are understood by all. They, and countless others like them, have been in our understanding since we were children. They are invaluable to the designer because a rapid translation of the information they contain relies on the eyes and not on speech.

Basic Costume

Basic costume describes a type of uniform dress that leaves the designer free to focus the audience's attention on small changes and accessories to denote the different characters. Black is often used – the black clothes that form the working uniform of youth theatre and student groups make it an easy option. It works well as a basic costume because the colour is neutral: beige, grey or cream, and even, on occasions, brown can all work just as well. Economy might demand that actors wear their own clothes as basic costume, leaving the accessories to be provided by the Wardrobe. When economy is not the driving factor, the design of the basic costume can be more closely allied to the spirit of the script.

There is a huge range of possibility. A play set in the Middle Ages could have all the men in tunic and tights and all the women in a longer version of the tunic. Detail would be added with headdresses and over-tunics, girdles and costume props. The colour or colours of the basic costume might be influenced by the plot and reflect the rich, glowing tones of a medieval Book of Hours, or the earthy shades of the agricultural field.

A post-modern production might call for the entire company to be barefoot in white underwear. Footwear, or lack of it, must always be considered when the basic costume is being designed, and, although bare feet may be the cheapest option, problems can arise. Slip-on shoes or slippers for

A neutral basic costume is dressed with sticks, helmets and belts. Photo: Robin Cottrell

backstage wear can avert accidents, but the set and backstage areas must be checked before each performance for nails and splinters.

Example

Imagine a group of actors in grey – grey shirts and trousers and skirts – and black shoes. None of the clothes gives particular information about time or status. They are just a group of men and women. They have to arrive at a chilly station by train. They all wear coats and scarves. Some are first-class passengers and some second. The first-class coats are fur, and the scarves soft wool and chiffon. The second-class passengers wear rougher wool coats and less opulent accessories. The tramp who huddles on the platform wears a ragged coat and pull-on hat; the porter wears a uniform jacket and cap. They all wear the basic costume underneath, and the audience can see parts of it inside or under the coats. But they will ignore it and take all their information about the characters onstage from their accessories, as well as from the way they talk and move and are grouped.

Costume for Dance

Costumes for dance cannot be designed in the same way as those for straight drama because of the way the movement and music encourages the watcher to interpret the work onstage. The movement of the cloth grabs the attention of the audience. They are engaged in a very visual experience and are consequently more aware of the flow or restrained behaviour of any fabric onstage. It calls for a particular skill from the designer and maker. The costumes have to be designed for movement. They have to fall back into place without being twitched or arranged by the dancer, and stay decent through the extremes of the highest arabesque.

The attention is focused on the body of the performer, and not on his or her voice. Think of a male and a female doing a back flip – the move when a performer springs into the air into a backbend, lands on their hands and flips upright again. Their first move is to stretch up their arms and bend slightly backwards. This pulls their costume upwards from the shoulders and tightens it all down the front of the body. The tendency of the costume is to ride up, taughten and display every detail of the body underneath. This may be fine, and, indeed, desirable in some performances, but other, less explicit shows will call for the security of dance supports for the men and suitable underwear or clever cutting of a low neck for woman, to avoid them ending up topless.

After the full backward stretch and somersault, the actor is upright again. Will the costume fall back to its original place, or will it clamp a Lycra second skin over the genitals, revealing embarrassing detail, or stay runkled and ugly on the body? Such practical problems are best tried out in the privacy of the Wardrobe before the more public exposure of the dress rehearsal.

Circus and Extreme Physical Performance

Circus costumes have to be practical enough to cope with the most extreme movement, and they also need to be safe. Traditional circus costume is bright and glittery, but in the 'new wave' circus of today, where a story may be suggested, harsh emotions may be explored, and lighting be more atmospheric, circus design is moving away from the dazzle of sequins and the impact of sharp colours towards more subtle effects. At the same time, the daring of the performers and the danger of their performances have increased. A flap of braid can catch on a wire or a button can dig into a fellow tumbler and ruin concentration or put a performer at risk.

Circus performers are used to danger, and know when some part on a costume constitutes a risk to their safety. Modern artistes are also increasingly audacious, always looking for new ways, physical and visual, to make their acts more exciting. The designer needs to listen hard at fittings; an experienced performer of any risky stunt will know more about possible dangers than you will. Allow time and space for them to check the safety of their costumes as thoroughly as they check their equipment.

You also need to be aware that the adrenaline of performance can overtake a performer's caution; the fire-juggler may not be aware of how close the flames lick to his cloak at the back, and the trapeze artist may not fully understand how a headdress moves as she somersaults high above the stage.

Youth Theatre and School Productions

Dressing up and putting on make-up is fun. If productions at school or in a youth theatre make an effort to costume the actors, they will be rewarded by an increased commitment and interest in all those involved. All actors find costume helps them with their role, and children are no exception. A costume does not have to be complicated to inspire a child. A tail and two ears on a headband, or a cloak made of a piece of cloth with two tapes to tie it on, can make a young child see themselves as a cat or Superman. Older children, once they have grasped the principle of adding accessories to basic costume, will begin to suggest the hats, scarves or shoes that will say something about the character they are playing.

When working with young people, it is a great help to appoint one person who will have an overview of all the costumes, particularly if every child is providing their own. A company left to itself, with no lead from a designer, may go onstage with some of the children beautifully dressed in imaginative and complete costumes, and others in ordinary clothes. A costume leader at the helm, who can guide costume discussions, make suggestions and help those who cannot get help at home, will smooth out the effect and create a design concept that will speak to the audience. As well as an ability to work with clothes and colours, the job also requires a degree of tact. Parents may make a huge effort with their child's costume, which, none the less, may be hopelessly inappropriate within the general style of the design.

'Design concept' sounds a bit formal, but it does not need to be complicated. It could be as simple as asking all the children to wear blue, white and black clothes (which most of them will be able to muster). This will leave a wide range of colours available to add as scarves, turbans, cloaks, or whatever is demanded by the story. Even such a simple organization will produce a more telling and deliberate picture onstage.

The group may have access to a collection of costumes that has been built up over the years. It is likely to be a pretty random bunch of dressing-up clothes, but it is not to be despised. Once again, with someone who leads the choice and keeps a balance in the style of the costume, it can provide a useful base, which can be added to for each production.

Youth and school productions may present all sorts of problems that could not possibly occur in a professional situation, and a number of compromises may have to be made. The children are not professionals; the audience will be made up of parents and friends, who will have different expectations from those of the critics, agents and paying theatregoers of London's West End. The most important thing is that everyone has the best experience they can in each circumstance; if everyone enjoys good design in the process, so much the better.

Costume for Student Performance

Students who are performing as part of a course of study need to understand costume. It is an essential part of many performances, but, until students are encouraged to look carefully at stage clothes, costumes may have only been noticed where they have been obvious. Romeo wears a costume; his doublet and hose have been designed and made by a costumier. The young lover in a modern television soap opera also wears a costume that is the work of a designer and maker. Students need to realize this, and to have an understanding of the effect that costume has on both the actor and the audience. There is a huge difference between dressing up – which is for the fun and enjoyment of the person wearing the costume – and wearing or making a costume whose purpose is to give information to the audience. Experiencing the use of costume for performance demonstrates the difference better than any lecture, class or book can.

A student performer can learn a huge amount in a costume fitting and in the discussions that precede the fitting. Budgets and facilities may make it impossible to provide costumes, but even a discussion of what would work if the money were available can be instructive. A good start is discussing the concept of the costume design with the whole group and explaining the sort of messages you hope your work will give the audience. Ask the group for ideas and talk about their reaction to your ideas. A professional actor will have past experience in the background; a student may never have worn or thought about costume before, or may have a limited knowledge from school or youth theatre.

Allow time at costume fittings with students for discussion and experiment. Encourage them to look at themselves in the mirror and see themselves as the audience will see them. Try and make time and space for them to move around in the costume, and to get a taste of the way the body is influenced by the clothes. Above all, make the occasion as relaxed and easy as you can, and make sure there is as little reserve as possible in communication between actor and fitter.

Carnival

Carnival costumes need to be bright and attention-grabbing and to have an instant impact. The person watching the carnival procession stands in

Making carnival costumes in the boiler room!

one place as the parade passes by; he has just one chance to see the costume, so there is no point in being too subtle. The lighting, usually in daylight in the open air, will be provided by the gods and not by the lighting designer, and colours have to shine through even when gods are frowning darkly.

Unless a very wealthy group is responsible for their creation, the makers of carnival costumes will be enthusiastic amateurs, with varying skills. Consequently, the design needs to be simple with immediate impact. Both the pattern and the instructions should be particularly clear and easy to understand. The makers and performers are working for fun, not money, and the design must make sure that there is opportunity for using the different levels of skill available. The sequins stuck on by a group of six-year-old children are as important to the finished effect as creating a structure for the giant wings of a bird. The effect of a float or group often relies on many people forming a block of moving colour or illustrating a theme, so the designer has to provide not only the

designs for the individual costumes, but also the way the costumed actors and dancers will be arranged to create the best effect on the street.

Shopping for cloth and decoration is best done by one person, with measured lengths being passed on to all the separate makers. It is usually possible to get a reduction when you buy in quantity, particularly where the quality of the cloth is not as important as its impact on the eye.

THE DESIGNS

You have studied the script and researched the appropriate background. The genre of the play, and the costume of the time, country, and class of the characters you will be dressing are clear in your head. Rough sketches and costume plot are to hand. You are ready to create, on the paper that lies ready on the table, a coloured image of every character in the play – with all their changes of clothes and accessories.

Presenting Your Designs

Methods
Your designs will help the company of directors, actors, lighters and makers to imagine the picture that will be presented to the audience on the first night. Of course, if you draw and paint beautifully, they may also be works of art, but that is not really the point. The point is to transfer the information from your brain to someone else's. A description, perhaps of colour, shape and texture, cannot, with any certainty, convey images that correspond to those in your imagination. However, even an inept sketch, perhaps with some fabric samples attached, will make it straightforward for people to understand the images of the costumes you hold in your head.

If you are designing costumes for the first time, it can feel as if your graphic skills are under the critical microscope, and you may find your imagination running ahead of your ability to draw and paint. Keep your head and remember that the drawings are only a backstage step to the final stage picture, as much a part of the working process as the early stages of rehearsal. It is bound to be nerve-wracking; it is always frightening to show the inside of your head to other people. It is also exciting and lucky to get the chance to make an imagined picture come to life.

There are absolutely no rules for presenting your ideas on paper. The conventional way is to draw and paint the costumed character on paper, with written notes, small sketches of details, and fabric samples included as added explanation. There are, however, other ways to proceed if you find it difficult to show what you mean in this way.

Photocopying or tracing images, which you can adapt and colour in, can free you from the need to draw. Search for an image that is close to the idea you have in mind. Blot out and alter parts you do not need, or want to change. Re-copy it,

adapt it and copy it again, until it gives an understandable representation of your concept for the costume. Throw away that hangover from school that you might be cheating by working in this way (although, of course, you must not plagiarize the works of others). You may find that, once you have played around with copies and adaptations, you have more confidence, and are able to draw a better and livelier design yourself than the one you have created from the copies.

Collage can be useful, as it creates a less naturalistic image and allows more freedom with the reality of the body. It is particularly useful to those who are more confident with the scissors than with the brush or pencil. Use coloured paper and cloth to build up the image of your costume design on strong paper. You may find that the detail

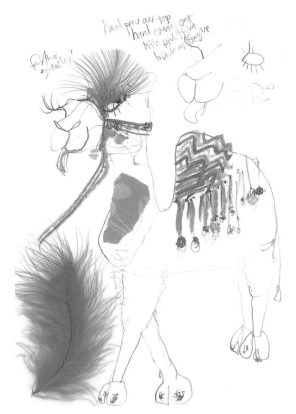

Designer James Randall uses collage, paint and pencil in these early working drawings for Camilla the Camel's costume.

can be added with pen or brush once the basic shapes have been set in place.

Small models can work well, and are particularly useful when designing transformations or costumes that adapt body shapes, or are worn by several actors at a time. A model gives you the opportunity to display practically how a cloak changes colour when worn in a different way, or how a costume reacts to UV light. It can be easier for people who are not used to looking at costume designs to understand a model, particularly if it is for a large-scale costume such as a giant, which might be worn by one actor sitting on another's shoulders, or a carnival costume that will be made by a group of amateur makers working together to create the effect.

It is not necessary to spend hours trying to get a face on your drawing to look right, unless you are designing a particular make-up, or to draw a beautiful hand, unless you are designing an elaborate glove. Search for a style of design that enables to you demonstrate your thoughts with the most freedom and clarity; you will find that, with

each attempt, you get better at showing an accurate picture of the concept in your mind. During the actual process of getting the idea on to the paper, concentrate on the character. Think about the way they feel and the way they talk and, even in cases when the designer has only a slight experience of drawing, the feeling of the character will come through in the design. It is hard to believe this if you have not experienced it, but it really is true; a deep understanding of the heart and soul of the people in the play is more important to the quality of the costumes than experience, money and skill.

Materials

Experiment with different methods until you find the one with which you feel most confident and easy. People who have the ideas, but are not used to drawing and painting, can become very tense and hunched over the process. If you recognize that feeling, you need to convince yourself that what you are doing is an unimportant experiment; use cheap paper that you can throw away as you go, or work on a long roll of wall-lining paper that does not have the formality of a sketch book. Try watercolours and crayons and pastels and inks, or anything you can get hold of in any combination. Quite quickly, you will find that you feel a preference for a particular medium, and when you have decided, buy the best possible version that you can afford. The same is true of paper. Some people are hampered by the feeling of working on expensive paper, while others are inspired by a thick, creamy or textured surface. Once again, there are no rules, beyond the practicality of size, finance and durability, so choose the paper that helps you to feel confident about your work.

A designer who does not make costumes can still find it useful to keep a supply of small samples of fabric, particularly if they will not be with the buyer on shopping trips. An example will demonstrate the texture and quality of cloth you have in mind and will speed up shopping. A designer who makes will build up a store, and the size of this store depends on the space available. Even a store that has to be crammed into a couple of boxes can be a great time-saver. In the hunt for

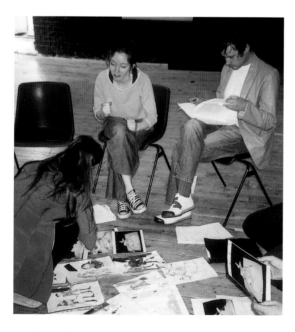

Costume designs may be referred to throughout rehearsal.

Example: Dressing the King

Creating the visual world of the play

Imagine you begin with the design for the King. As you begin to trust your ideas to the paper, the visual world you are making develops a crisp reality. The vague conceptions that can be skimmed over in your thoughts demand to be filled in when they appear as gaps on paper. You may have pictured the King's robe and crown but what else does he wear – trousers? Knee-breeches? How are they kept up – a belt? A sash? Braces? Does he wear a shirt and waistcoat or a tunic? What sort of buttons? Which medals? A sword? What is round his neck – a tie? A cravat? A mandarin collar? Does he have a beard or is he clean-shaven? Shoes, socks? Gloves?

Reference to the costume plot and set design will produce more queries. Does he have a quick change? Will his waistcoat and trousers be worn under a different coat in another scene? What fabric upholsters the throne he will sit on? What colour are the background and hangings of the throne-room scene? The answers to all these questions, and more, will be reflected in your costume design.

Balancing the power of the characters

This King is starting to appear on the paper. Think back to the script. How does he affect the scene in which he wears this costume? Should he be the focus of the audience's attention and draw every eye? Or is he merely observing the interaction between two of his courtiers, who, although lesser creatures in the court, are more important to the plot? If so, his costume, and the way it is lit, must not distract the audience's attention. What about his Queen? Should one of them be the more dominant character or are they equal partners?

Demonstrating character

This King has to look kingly in a way that is appropriate to the period of the play, and the formal court scene in the script demands regal robes. The designer must find the trick of demonstrating the character of the man beneath the clothes. He may be a splendid King – a noble, virile King Arthur at the height of his power, wearing his heavy robes with casual grace – or he may be the weedy, peevish Dauphin, whose shoulders sag under the weight of his overlong, trailing robe as he faces St Joan. The costume must help the actor inhabit the body of the character. Any actor will tell you the boost that a costume that feels right gives to their performance and most will have had experience of costumes that are obstructive to the physicality demanded by a role.

supplies for each project, you will come across unusual items or bargains which are bound to be useful and each project will leave part finished reels of thread and odds and ends of haberdashery which will always be useful. There is always a balancing act between the storage space available and the wish to hold on to things for future use.

A4 is a practical paper size for costume designers, but if you find it too small there is nothing to stop you working on larger paper. It must be possible to spread the designs out and shuffle their position on a table during discussions and meetings, so the drawings should be on separate sheets rather than contained in a sketch book. You can always file them in clear envelopes for convenient reference when shopping, and unclip them when you need to look at all the images together. They will be passed round and handled by lots of people during the production period and must be sturdy enough to stand up to this. The fabric samples should be attached securely to the drawings; they still tend to come adrift during their working life, which is another good reason for containing each design in a transparent cover.

Copies can be made for costume makers or anyone one else who needs to have the designs at hand for reference. Remember that the copyright of the drawings remains the property of the designer, and permission must be obtained if they are to be reproduced for publicity or programme material.

Lighting

The mood of the scene, as much as the supposed time of day and place, will influence the design of the lighting and you must take this into consideration with your choice of colour and texture. It is unlikely that you will know in advance the exact lighting state under which your costumes will appear, but you can get a general idea from the script. If you do get the opportunity to talk to the lighting designer at an early stage of the design process, grab it, and use it to discuss colours and moods of scenes. Are you both working towards the same goal? Perhaps the fabric you want to use for a king's robes will gleam particularly richly in a golden, rather than a steely light. A chat at the right time may make a difference to the lighting plot, which could not be made at a later stage, and allow the costume to be seen at its best.

The way the costumes are lit onstage has as much effect on them as the way they are worn by the actors. It is worth learning as much as you can about how lighting works on fabrics and noticing the way costumes appear when moving in different lighting states. Rig a test light in your workroom, if you have the space. You can get sample books of different-coloured gels to test the effects that light colours have on cloth; lighting designers often have spare books that they may pass on to you, while firms who supply lighting effects give them away free.

Sampling

Sampling is the collection of samples of textiles appropriate to each costume. Very large companies may have someone whose job it is to collect such samples for the designer's approval. A designer working with a costume supervisor may either trust their judgement enough to leave them to choose and buy the cloth, or may accompany the supervisor or maker trekking round shops and suppliers to find the appropriate cloth, braid and buttons.

It is not a simple matter of choosing; there are other questions to be considered. The picture to be created onstage is, of course, at the forefront of every decision. However, the yardage and the budget also have to be considered with every purchase, in conjunction with the practicality of the fabric for the purpose. The exhausting shopping sprees involve a complicated balancing act, which has to maintain a triangle of practicality, cost and desirability.

The Complete Set of Designs

When the file of designs is complete, every costume worn by every character will be illustrated, and many of them will have scraps of cloth attached. The designs can be scanned and sent via the internet, and stored on a CD. If the CD is to be used for display at production meetings, make sure that the hardware will be available when and where you want it.

One way of testing the efficiency of your design is by imagining you are trying to make it without talking to the designer. It should be possible for cutters and makers in the workroom to transfer the idea from the flat piece of paper to the moving body without further explanation, although, in practice they will be able to ask questions. Makers, particularly if they work for film or television, are used to being given pages from magazines, real clothes to copy, or downloaded information from the web from which to work. Nothing, however, communicates an idea better on paper than a good drawn and painted design; as well as the shape and colour of the actual clothes, the feeling that the designer has for the character is also transferred through brush and pencil, conveying an emotional as well as a visual message.

Design for Low-Budget Production

It is an expensive matter to design and make the costumes for a performance from scratch. If you roll the jobs of designer, costume supervisor or shopper, and maker into one, the benefit to the budget is more than the sum of the wages. Extra makers may be needed but the shopping bill can be cut dramatically, because the designs can be built up at the same time as the samples and, in some cases, the cut and colour of the clothes can be adapted to suit the cloth available. If you are working in a small and impoverished company, it is by far the best way to produce a professional effect that shows no signs of its humble background and sings out with all the power that an integrated design base gives to a production. This is how you do it.

Read the script, then research and draw without colour all the costumes as if you had enough money to do whatever you wanted. Make a separate sheet of painted colour patches of the tones and shades that you imagined throughout the drawing process.

After this stage, you can begin to shop, but this time with the budget firmly in your mind, alongside the feeling that you are building the picture gradually. Try not to get too set on finding an exact match to your imagined picture, and be prepared to shift your ideas if an unexpected colour or texture sparks something in your imagination. You will probably be searching in markets and car-boot, jumble and garage sales rather than department stores and smart fabric shops, where the prices will be higher. Stock will tend to be jumbled rather than displayed neatly in clear rows of colour, texture and price. You may well unearth, on a heaped market stall, a worn dress of useless shape and colour, which is bordered with a braid that can be ripped off and used to splendid effect on a coat. It might seem an extravagance to buy a dress that you are going to chuck in the bin, but compare the cost (in time and money) with tracking down and buying a similar braid in a shop. You can always keep a huge bag on the go for the cloth recycling depot if you feel guilty of waste.

Your first shopping trip may yield enough cloth for the heroine's dress and an old curtain, which, when unpicked and washed, will be just the right colour and texture for the coat to go over the dress; moreover, the curtain may have a lining that is the oatmeal colour and worn texture you had imagined for the loyal servant's blouse. On another stall you may find a waistcoat, which can be altered slightly to make it look Edwardian, and a couple of collarless shirts, for which you can cut new collars from the shirt tails. Perhaps a bag of buttons and braid and lace scraps, which will be useful somewhere, might be added to the shopping bag.

Searching through the scrap basket for useful fabric.

When you get back to your workroom and spread out your booty, you can paint in the colours of the dresses of the heroine and her mother, the servant's blouse, and the hero's waistcoat, and attach samples of your purchases to the designs so that you will have the colours with you on your next shopping trip. Re-evaluate your designs. Perhaps now that the colours of two of the women's dresses have been decided, the loyal servant should be in a darker colour than the one you first imagined? Perhaps the colour of the hero's waistcoat should be reflected in the braid or accessories of his beloved? Perhaps the sleeves of the mother's dress will need to be re-designed so that they can be cut in two sections and use less material? You can respond to these decisions immediately when you are both designing and shopping, and adjust the complete picture of the designs as you go along, without losing sight of your original concept.

47

1 Skirt in stock but too short for actress. Change of bodice colour.

2 Actress has short hair, which necessitates either wig or different headdress. Skirt let down at waist.

3 Bodice redesigned with peplum to disguise that it has been let down from the waist.

4 Finished design.

Shopping changes for the maidservant — the gradual build-up of a costume.

The advantages and disadvantages of this method of working balance each other. Its success depends on your interest in the thrill of the shopping chase as well as your ability to judge how much and what type of fabric will be needed for each costume, and to make a good guess at the way a costume will be cut. Costume designers vary in their knowledge of cutting and making, and this method becomes a rather risky gamble when the designer, having shopped, passes on bundles of cloth and clothes to a maker.

It is possible that an idea may arise, inspired by a particular purchase, that makes a considerable difference to a concept for a costume that has been agreed at an earlier stage of the process. In this case, the change should be discussed with the director before the decision is finalized.

Most productions, in their design as well as rehearsal, are part of a growing process and subject to change in many directions in the early stages. It is productive to keep ideas fluid for as long as possible – as long as the lines of communication to all company members who might be affected by the ideas are kept open. Lack of departmental communication may lead to an actress in a beige dress delivering the most important speech of the play on a beige upholstered sofa in beige lighting – with the audience watching in a beige fug of inattention.

4 THE WARDROBE

WARDROBES AND WORKROOMS

The Wardrobe, or costume workshop, is the place where the costumes are made, fitted and looked after. Wardrobes vary as much as productions. They range from the splendidly equipped, clean workroom with rows of cutting tables, sewing machines and pressing stations, to the cramped room with one machine, a table and an ironing board. Most are something in between. They will all have sewing and ironing equipment, as well as other bits: bits of cloth, bits of haberdashery, a mirror and more boxes; belts and ribbons and gloves; shelves of dyes and thread and tools. And there will always be someone, or a group of people, who work in them, and know and love every scrap, thread and mitten in the place.

Organizing Your Hoard

You cannot make costumes for long without learning the value of hoarding. You soon learn the hours and hours that can be saved by having a length of gold cord, left over from a previous production, that is just long enough to outline the base of a crown. The most important thing is not so much the money you save by not having to buy the cord, but the fact that you do not have to stop work to go out and shop. As soon as you find that bit in your hoard, you can finish off the crown, cross it off your list and get on with the next job. Disorderly hoarding is useless. Your hoard is disorderly if it takes longer for you to find the item than it would to go and buy it. It is vital to create some sort of system of organization. If you do not use and replenish the hoard it may be a sign that you are becoming a collector rather than a creator of costumes.

Basics

Haberdashery, thread and tape, binding and needles will all be in daily use. Even if you are working on different jobs for different companies in one workroom, haberdashery becomes a common resource; it is just too complicated to separate the cost of leftovers. There will leftovers from every job and it is sensible to buy elastic, bias binding, neutral colours of thread, and so on, in larger quantities, because it is cheaper and more

Some of the Wardrobe's hoard.

convenient. The cost can be divided between jobs if necessary.

Ribbons

You have to work out a storage system that suits your stock and space. You may, for example, have enough room to have a whole cupboard devoted to different colours and textures and widths of ribbon. Or you may have an empty shoe box with scraps and odd lengths gleaned from birthday wrappings and past hats. In either case, the hoard, cupboard or shoebox will be labelled 'Ribbon', and you will have a pretty good idea of what is in it. Even those wardrobe people who have an entire cupboard housing a hundred rolls of assorted ribbons will still save the birthday stuff if it is a good or useful colour.

Buttons

A few single buttons are useful, but buttons should be hoarded in sets, rather than singly. It can take much longer to make up a more-or-less matching set of buttons from a random collection than it will to go to a shop and buy new ones. A button collection, or a boxful of muddled threads that has become unmanageable, is best organized by a child who enjoys sorting; keep your eyes open for a possible interested helper.

Cloth

Everyone can find space for a store of haberdashery, but not everyone has space to store cloth. When space is very limited you will have to be strict with yourself and keep only pieces that you know you will use as linings or stiffening, although you will find it impossible not to hoard a few pieces of irreplaceable or particularly lovely scraps. There are some fabrics that will be used in every show: lining material in neutral colours, white and black cotton fabric, stiffening and interlining. Try to find the space and money to keep a stock of these essential supplies at hand. The rest depends on the amount of storage space you have at your disposal. Every project will leave a pile of remnants in the Wardrobe and almost everything could be used in time, so you have to decide if you would rather have the space or the cloth.

Costumes

The same is true of costumes. It can be a wonderful saving of both time and money when the company has a stock of costumes, particularly if they are clean, well organized and in relatively strong condition. Once again, where there is not room to store everything, hold on to the smaller items. Tights, hats, aprons, gloves will all be used over and over again and will not be recognized by the audience in the way that a costume they have seen in a previous production may be. Shoes take up a lot of space, but they also use up a lot of the budget. Keep them if you can, particularly if they are in reasonable condition and would be expensive or difficult to replace.

The Theatre Wardrobe

All large-scale theatres and theatres that mount in-house productions, have a Wardrobe, usually at the top of flights of stone stairs. Equipment varies but there will be sewing machines, irons and tables, and access to washing and drying facilities. If you are lucky there will be excellent light, a good store of haberdashery and cloth, an overlocker and an industrial sewing machine, and an easily accessible store of costumes and accessories. If you are unlucky it will be an airless room, with just enough space to work if you keep the clothes rail on the landing outside, and a fifteen-minute walk down the road to a launderette. Costume makers are used to improvization and many marvellous costumes have been cut out on the floor for want of a cutting table, dyed and painted in a backyard by the scene dock, and sewn on a machine balanced on a wobbly trestle table. It is not ideal; quite often, half a day's work with a helpful stage manager and an extension lead will improve the facilities, stop the tables wobbling, add more light and power points and make life much easier in the Wardrobe.

Setting up a Workroom

You may be working in a rehearsal building or a theatre that does not have a permanent room for the Wardrobe. Your temporary workroom may be in a dressing room, a spare rehearsal space or even a tent if the production is in the open air. You will need to set up the Wardrobe in this space as best you can, making the most of its advantages and working round any drawbacks. It is worth taking time to get it right, particularly if you know you will be working in it for some time and using it for fittings and storing the completed costumes until they go to the dressing rooms for the tech. A project is more likely to run smoothly if the workroom is as convenient as you can make it. There is quite a long list of things to consider:

Power You will need to plug in equipment. Try to arrange things so that cables are at the back of tables and not running across the floor space. Tape hazardous cables to the floor so that you do not take a pratfall over them when your arms are full of costumes. An extension lead and an adaptor are a useful standby in the toolbox; there are always lots of them about in theatre buildings, but they are always difficult to track down. Public buildings have safety regulations, and an electricity supply that cuts out more easily than a domestic one; if you have doubts or problems, check with the production manager, stage manager or whoever is in charge of safety in the building. There is lots of flammable stuff in a Wardrobe. Make sure that you can find the fire exits, and that they are unlocked. Check the rules on emergency procedure, as the safety of anyone in the Wardrobe, as well as your own, may be your responsibility if the fire alarm rings.

Light You need to have good light by which to work. Natural light is the most restful but it is not necessary as the costumes will always be seen onstage in artificial light. Position tables to catch the best of the light. Make sure that your working position does not keep the light off your work. If necessary, ask for extra, temporary lighting. You may be working long hours and you will work with more energy in a bright room. Make sure that light sources are kept well clear of the work; it does not take long for a piece of filmy veiling to start singeing on a dressing room light.

Sewing machines Reliability and strength are more important than a wonderful range of

A makeshift cutting table in a dressing room.

embroidery stitches. Sewing machines in theatres are required to sew leather and foam, net and gauze, and heavy scenic canvas. Oil and service machines regularly, change the needle often and learn how to use any attachments. Make sure the machine does not move about on the table with the vibration of sewing. A non-slip mat or a blob of blue-tack under each corner will sort out any problem.

Iron and ironing board You will use the iron constantly when you are making and it needs to be positioned so that it is convenient and close to the work tables. A tape attached to a hook in the ceiling that is just long enough to keep the iron off the floor if it gets knocked off its perch may save several irons. A sleeve board – a small board that sits on top of the ironing board and allows you to press narrow sleeves, or any other tubular piece of costume – can be a great help. A padded wodge of cloth, about the size of a large hamburger, can be used as a sort of portable ironing support for hats and shoulder seams and other awkward rounded shapes. Make sure the ironing board is set at a comfortable height to avoid back-ache.

Tables The best cutting table is at the right height to allow you to work standing without stooping, and big enough to spread out lengths of the widest cloth for cutting. If you are setting up a temporary workroom, you will probably have to make do with something less convenient. Two standard trestle tables set in a square shape is a good substitute. One by itself is manageable, but rather narrow, and you will have to cut larger items on the floor. Machine tables need space on the left of the machine to support the work. Take the trouble to adjust the height of tables and chairs until you are comfortable. Costumes can be heavy to work on and hours may be long. The right ratio of chair height to table height will make a lot of difference to your staying power.

Mirrors There should be a full-length mirror so that actors can see themselves in their costumes at fittings. A mirror is a great help to a maker working in a small space. They make it possible for you to view the actor in costume from a greater

An actor discusses the comedy value of his costume at a fitting.

distance, as you add his distance from the reflection to your distance from the mirror. The reflection you see is two-dimensional, rather than three-dimensional, and this gives you a clear view of your work and enables you to pinpoint mistakes in a way that can be difficult in reality.

Materials and haberdashery stock You will need shelves or a spare table (or even a board across a couple of chairs) to stack your fabric where you can see it, as well as a reasonably organized place for haberdashery and bits and pieces. The organization of this area becomes particularly important when there is more than one worker in the space. There has to be a place for everything so that all the makers know where to find thread and buttons and tapes, and know where to put them back when they have finished.

Accessory store Accessories such as hats, boots, daggers and handkerchiefs can be organized in boxes or bins and shoved under the cutting table when they are not needed. There should also be a few boxes for scraps and offcuts of cloth, which should never be thrown out until the show is complete; even after the end of the show, it is worth reserving a few bits for repairs and patching.

Rubbish A lot of stuff in the Wardrobe looks like rubbish to the uninitiated. Anyone who has left on the floor a bin liner full of carefully dyed rags to make the beggar's costume and found, the next morning, that the bag has vanished into the dustbin lorry will know the value of a loud-labelled rubbish bin. Even when cleaners are employed to clear up every day, it is a good idea to have a broom and sweep the rubbish into a pile each night; there is no visible difference to anyone but the cutter between the carefully cut collar squeezed out of the last offcuts of cloth and dropped on the floor by mistake, and a useless lappet discarded on purpose.

In addition to this list, there are many other things that will make your life easier. These non-essential items might include dressmaking dummies, wig blocks and hat stands, running water and a sink, an overlocking machine, a comfortable temperature, a changing room, a separate area for painting and dyeing, and an office corner with a computer and telephone. The greatest help of all is space, which is nearly always in short supply. There is never enough, but a kettle, a packet of biscuits and a supply of fruit can diffuse many difficult situations. A happy, friendly Wardrobe draws and comforts the company like the kitchen table in a house.

Working in the Wardrobe

You may be working alone, or you may be one of a team of designers, cutters, makers, dyers, and shoppers. Some people are tidy workers, who work their way steadily and efficiently through a list of tasks at a work table that is always orderly and calm. Others work most happily in a morass of thread and scraps, with their lunch muddled up with the lace. Both ways of working are perfectly valid providing they come up with the goods, but the two approaches do not mix on one table. Try to make sure everyone in the team has their own space, which they can organize to suit themselves. It is easy for the wardrobe department to forget that their workroom is also a place of work for the actors. Costume fittings are an important part of the character-building process that an actor goes through when creating a role. The Wardrobe should be a friendly, unthreatening place that welcomes actors – not a place where they feel rushed, unwelcome or uneasy.

TOOLS AND THEIR USE

The sewing machine and iron are the biggest items in the costume maker's toolbox, but there are many more. You will collect your own as you go along, but below is a list of the most essential; if this is your first job, you may not have thought of some of them.

Cutting scissors Buy the best dressmaking shears you can afford. Test before you buy that they feel comfortable in your hand and are not too heavy to manipulate with accuracy. Keep them for your own use and only use them for cloth, as paper or card, or anything else, will blunt them. It takes

practice to cut a smooth, straight line, and to have the confidence to cut boldly so that you are almost drawing a line with your scissors. The instinct to be careful can make you hunch close and tense over the work and the line you are cutting will be jagged.

Small scissors These should be sharp-pointed, for trimming threads, cutting buttonholes and carrying out small light work. Again, the sharper the better. It is also useful to have a pair to use on the move at dress rehearsals; these should have round points, so that you can keep them in your pocket without stabbing your thigh.

Rough work scissors Keep these for cutting paper, card, foam and anything that might blunt your best pairs.

Lending scissors People always come to the Wardrobe to borrow scissors and having a spare pair to lend will save you raging round the theatre trying to reclaim them, when you need to get on with your work.

Pencils, marker pens, tailor's chalk Pencil works clearly on fabric but may show on a light one. Pens show up better as long as the marks they leave will not be visible to the audience, or run in the wash. Tailor's chalk or dressmaker's pencil (from haberdashery shops) will not leave a permanent mark.

Pins Extra-long good-quality dressmaker's pins are the best for general theatre use. They are more secure for fittings and easier to use than the shorter ones. The pins with coloured plastic heads are easy to pick up but can mark the fabric if the plastic head is touched by a hot iron. Very cheap pins can be too thick and blunt to get into the fabric easily.

Self-stick labels These are endlessly useful, particularly if you are cutting a lot of costumes that look the same.

Needles (machine and hand sewing) You can buy special bladed needles for machine and hand sewing, which make the job of sewing leather easier. You will use more thick needles than you would for dressmaking. You will also break quite a lot, so keep a reserve stock. You will also need hand-sewing needles that will take thin string or ribbon on occasions and extra-long needles for hats and wadding.

Metre/yard rule and tape measure A tape with metres on one side and inches on the other is the best option.

Paintbrushes These will be used for applying glue, as well as paint, and you will need both fine and thick, for mask work and shoes, and so on.

Crochet hook One end will be used for hooking, the other for wiggling out the points of collars or turning tubes of cloth inside-out.

Rouleaux turner Available from haberdashery shops, this is a 25-cm (10-in) wire with a latchet on one end and a loop on the other. It is actually made for turning very fine rouleaux or tubes of cloth, but has all sorts of other uses, such as hooking out a waist elastic that has vanished into a waistband.

Other useful tools include the following:

- pliers with wire cutter;
- long-nosed pliers for jewellery;
- awl or hole punch;
- tack hammer;
- small saw;
- assorted safety pins;
- clipboard or notebook;
- extension lead;
- plug adaptor;
- spray bottle, for damping cloth and stretching hats;
- masking tape and gaffer tape;
- clothes brush;
- comb for ironing fringe as well as for preparing wigs;
- clock or watch with second hand for timing quick changes;

- door wedge – there will be frequent occasions when you do not have a hand spare to hold the door open.

WORKING ON THE COSTUMES

Interpreting the Drawings
A discussion usually has to take place between the designer and the cutter and maker, if only to make sure that all the information in the drawing has been understood. This will be an exchange of purely technical information about the fullness of gathers or the placing of seams, but there may be other problems that are not obvious in the drawing, which will become apparent when the design has become a real costume on a real actor. Perhaps the design is for a close-fitting early nineteenth-century coat. The script calls for the actor to be ambushed and to swing himself out of danger on to a balcony on the set. The cutter may foresee that such a closely cut coat will prevent the actor from reaching above his head for his athletic swing. He might be forced to scramble unromantically up a convenient drainpipe, or to take his coat off, which would make him appear to be expecting the ambush. The cutter will know that the coat must be cut with deeper armholes, slightly fuller sleeves and a more generous waist measurement, to allow free movement. A moment discussing this potential problem before the coat is cut, will potentially save a solid day's work for the Wardrobe, a hold-up at the technical rehearsal for director and actors, and much longer discussion for everybody.

Some designers have every smallest detail, each button and pocket flap, and the exact sweep of each seam, clear in their mind and in their drawings. Others design a general effect, and leave the details to the cutter and maker. Makers must understand the way their designer works, and clarify exactly how they expect the designs to be interpreted. The budget may be a deciding factor in many of these discussions. The Wardrobe may have a shirt, blouse, shoes or some other part of the

OPPOSITE: Costume design with notes for the maker.

High Spin
'Who Dunnit?'

Hat to 'friske'
off for
dance.

Skirt cut
double circle.

Poss. with black
top & yellow
gloves for change

black net
underskirt &
black pants for
upside-down moments.

T.B.

The Princess's Sister.

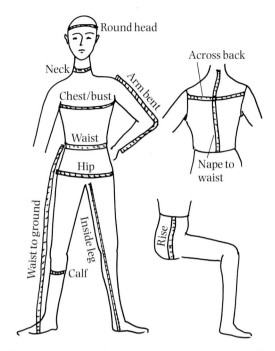

The most essential measurements. Shoe size will also be needed. Many people are not sure where to take a waist measurement particularly if they wear low-slung trousers or skirts; the safest way to find the spot is to tie a tape or string round the thinnest part of the body.

costume in their stock. It may not be exactly the same as the design, but it might do, and represent a considerable saving of time and money. Compromises may have to be made on both sides. To reproduce every item of clothing exactly as it appears in the design is a very expensive luxury and one that can usually only be afforded by rich companies.

Cutting

The job of the cutter is to cut the fabric to the shape of the design and to the measurements of the actor who is playing the role. Different cutters like working from slightly different lists of measurements, and experience will have taught them to allow for some inaccuracies in the measurements they are given, unless they have taken them themselves. Actor's agents have a list of

their client's measurements, which they send out, but they may have been taken some years before and not give an accurate, current picture. Actors, like most other people, are usually trying to get fitter and leaner, so their measurements change and are sometimes affected by optimism.

The person cutting the costumes may not be the person who makes them. When cutter and maker work together regularly, they will develop shorthand of chalk marks and notches in the fabric, which save discussion in the making of each costume. They will know each other's style of work and recognize the little signs. Pieces should be labelled if they might be difficult to recognize – a breeches knee band might be mistaken for a stand-up collar, for example – and it may need to be made clear which side of the fabric will show. It is not unusual for a designer to choose a cloth for the look of the wrong, rather than the right, side of the fabric. A short discussion when the cut pieces are handed over helps prevent mistakes in the making.

Making

The maker who is not cutting is presented with a pile of cut pieces. It will help the maker's understanding of how this little heap turns into a dress or suit if she has a drawing, even if it is only a black and white photocopy of the original design. The first thing to sort out is which side of the cloth is to be used as the right side, and which piece is which. The drawing helps to identify, for example, a gathered sleeve or a two-piece fitted sleeve, or whether a bodice is cut in shaped sections or fitted with darts. The maker will need to see a picture in her mind of the whole costume before she can determine the order of putting the pieces together.

The easiest way into the project may be to make up a sleeve or a collar to get the feel of the cloth – how it sews and how it behaves under the iron. An offcut of cloth should always be used to check the way temperature and steam affect the cloth; a fabric may look like wool or cotton but have threads of fibre lurking in its weave which will shrivel and crinkle under a hot iron. Where there are likely to be alterations at fittings, such as the armhole or the centre-back, a long machine stitch will make it easy to unpick and reset the seam.

There are times when it will be easier to apply braid or appliqué work before the garment is made up. If, for instance, you are working on a sleeve with a narrow cuff and military stripes of gold braid, it will be more practical to stitch on the braid while the seam is flat and sew the sleeve seam afterwards. In this case, of course, any alterations to the sleeve length would be made by re-cutting the top of the sleeve, rather than at the hem (as would be usual).

The garment will be made ready for a fitting, at which point it can be checked and adjusted, and lengths determined and marked. The actor will have the first inkling of the way his or her costume will move and how it will feel. It helps a lot if the designer can be present at these early fittings; details of decoration and anything that jars in the shape and the fit of the costume can be put right more quickly and easily at this stage than when the costume is complete. It can happen that an actor finds the costume difficult to wear, or feels either that it looks dreadful and they could hardly face going on stage in it, or that it does not sit comfortably with the interpretation of the character that is growing in rehearsal. The maker can do little more than adjust the fit of the costume; only the designer can make a dramatic change in the concept of the costume. Any such problems tend to grow as the first night looms, and it is much better to sort them out early, although the temptation may be to skirt round the issue and hope it fades away.

THE WARDROBE TEAM

Work Experience
Wardrobe departments may be asked if they will include in their team a student who needs to gain work experience. This can be dull and unrewarding for both parties, but sometimes it may lead to an exciting new career and a future working partnership. You do not know which until you try. In the worst case, you will be lumbered with a star-struck youngster who thinks that working in the theatre is glamorous and fun, and expects to be plucked from the Wardrobe to a role in the spotlight. From the student's point of view,

she may see herself lumbered with two weeks of sewing on hooks and eyes and sweeping the floor and making tea.

It does not have to be like that. A young person who shows an interest in Wardrobe work can prove a real godsend in the busy workroom. Finding time to teach an inexperienced helper is difficult and it may seem easier to give them undemanding work. But if you take the trouble to find out their interests, to encourage them to be present at fittings, and show them the skills they need to be a real help, you may be quickly rewarded for your patience. You may discover an unexpected ability that will save you hours and give them a taste, as they feather a hat or paint a mask, of the excitement of creating costumes.

Try to provide your young assistant with as varied and interesting a programme as they can cope with. Make sure that they are able to see some of the tech and the dress rehearsal, and that they have the opportunity to gain a first-hand experience of how a theatre company works together to create a production. You will

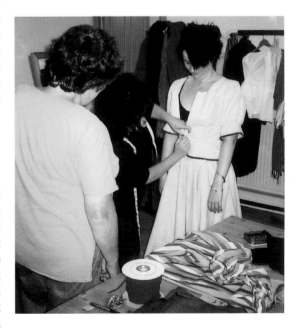

Designer, maker and actor work together at a fitting.

sometimes be asked for a report on their work and should be prepared for a workroom visit from a tutor or teacher.

WORKING ALONE

You may be designer, cutter, maker and everything else, and be creating the costumes by yourself. In some ways, this makes things easier. You can decide how you want things to look and have much more freedom to change your mind. You do not have to wait for design decisions and can work closely with the actors to balance their confidence in their costumes with the picture you have in your mind. You can judge how much time the work will take and do not have the responsibility of keeping a workroom happy and productive.

On the down side, you will have no one to share the problems with and encourage you through bad patches – it can help to have someone to work with, if the budget can cope. There are times when you really need an extra pair of hands or another eye and opinion, and it is rare to find two Wardrobe workers who have exactly the same strengths and weaknesses. It is good if you share equal commitment to getting the work done and there is no comfort like exchanging a secret look at a difficult fitting, sharing a bar of chocolate after a disastrous bit of cutting, or laughing at the same jokes.

Attitude

As in every department of a theatre company, the communication between designers, cutters and makers, and understanding and respect for each other's ideas, are the elements that make the work rewarding and exciting – and successful. Everybody has to want to make the finished product as good as possible, and creating this atmosphere in the Wardrobe is a skill in itself, perhaps more important than the best training and experience. Nobody can create good work in an antagonistic, pessimistic, defeatist atmosphere. Wardrobes often become a battlefield, where the staff feel unappreciated and both designer and actors have to brace themselves each time they approach the door.

This situation is fostered when the members of the wardrobe department is working away from the rest of the company, and feel their work is unappreciated. Many directors rarely visit the Wardrobe to chat about how the work is going, and find it hard to spare actors from a busy rehearsal schedules for fittings. The costume department do not see enough of rehearsals to have a close understanding of the style of performance and rehearsal, and communications and helpfulness between stage management and the Wardrobe are strained. Wardrobes really do have a similar place as the kitchen in a family home – when the atmosphere in the Wardrobe is tense, this will be reflected in the comfort and confidence of the actors.

Actors see themselves as part of the whole production in rehearsal, but in the Wardrobe, where they come by themselves to create the visual picture the audience will see of their character, they are in a vulnerable position. It is difficult for them to see themselves as a small part of a larger onstage picture. Many actors will have had past experience of a miserable time working in a confidence-sapping costume they hated wearing, and they will expect the worst, and be prepared to fight to be comfortable and feel they look right. On the other side of the fence are the Wardrobe staff, most of whom have their own past experience of troublesome actors, who demanded constant attention and did not seem to realize how much work it takes to make changes to a costume and how little time there is to do it. When the situation is unhappy like this (and it happens all too often), it is because both parties have forgotten that they are on the same side of the fence, working towards the same objective: giving the best experience to the audience.

The leader of the Wardrobe team is the person most responsible for creating a good working atmosphere and nothing helps more than mutual respect, a sense of humour, and biscuits.

OPPOSITE: *Kevork Malikyan as Estragon, Bruce Purchase as Pozzo, Nadim Sawalha as Vladimir and Ben Daniels as Lucky in* Waiting for Godot. *Photo: Robbie Jack*

5 SHOPPING

WHERE AND HOW TO SHOP

The way you shop for each production depends on the amount of money you have to spend and the amount of time you have to spend it. It is not particularly difficult to find just what you want if you have a generous budget and plenty of time. You can go to specialist shops and specialist suppliers, and if they do not have what you want you can get it made. Shoes can be made to your design and fabric specially woven and printed. However, it is unlikely that you will be reading this book if you have lots of money at your disposal and can buy as much expert help as you need. This is advice for those who are working on a smaller budget and need help to find the best suppliers for their productions.

Fabric

The perfect fabric shop, where everything you want is in one place at the right price in sufficient quantity, does not exist. Some do come very close, however, getting the atmosphere right as well as stocking the right sort of fabric. The process of creating costume is an emotional one, as subject to atmosphere as writing or painting or acting. There are shops that specialize in theatrical fabrics and trimmings, staffed by people who have experience of interpreting designs and advising on suitable fabrics and quantities. They are often familiar with the needs of theatrical designers and well informed about how the fabric will react to light, wear and movement. They may even have an ultraviolet

OPPOSITE: Saffron Burrows as Janey Morris and Nigel Lindsay as William Morris in Earthly Paradise. *Photo: Robbie Jack*

light available for testing the reaction of different fabrics. Prices in this kind of shop will not be cheap and it may not be as good, either for your style of costumes or for your budget, as a more friendly but less specialized place, where the staff know the sort of thing you look for, the sort of money you are likely to spend and the way you work.

A shop that suits your style of design can be an inspiration, as well as providing the most practical, down-to-earth help. You will need time to think, to wander round with your file of drawings, to ask for help to find a particular type of fabric. You will need to feel free to unroll a length of cloth to see

---

Extras

Choosing the fabric and trimmings to make the costume is only part of the story. Wigs, hats, footwear and costume props all need to be bought, too, and can often soak up as much of the budget as the dress or suit, or perhaps even more. The cloth is usually bought first, so it is essential to be careful enough to have funds in hand for these expensive extras. They may look small on your drawing, and seem to be less important than the main part of the costume, but in the onstage light, the whole effect will be spoiled by shortcomings of hairstyles or inappropriate shoes or stockings. You do not want to draw attention away from everything else that you have worked so hard to create. A really good costume can seem so natural to the character that it goes unnoticed; mistakes, even if they are small in relation to the whole costume, draw the eye like a boil on the nose.

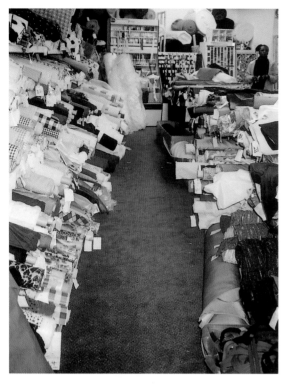

The mixture of colour and texture in the fabric shop gives inspiration to a designer.

how it hangs, to shine a torch on its texture to see how it reacts to artificial or UV light, and to cut small samples to compare with other bales of cloth.

Through regular buying trips you should build up a relationship with the staff of such a shop; they will begin to know what you like, and may give excellent advice on alternatives and particular bargains. As an extra bonus (which may rescue you in those dread moments when you are sitting at your work table stuck for an idea), you will feel welcome to wander through the shop's range of colours, with no particular end in view. An impromptu trip might well reset you on the path to a fresh idea and unblock the dam in your mind.

Trimmings

Braid, ribbons and other bits and bobs can form a substantial part of the design. They are the punctuation marks in a costume, which point out information to the audience. It is easy to overlook the time it may take to track them down and the amount of money they will cost. A long scarlet feather and some 'jet' buttons may be the only decoration on a black costume, but the feather must be a clear scarlet and substantial enough to

The expert and expensive work of creating a fabric to a design.

show from the furthest seat in the auditorium, while the buttons, even though they are really plastic, must catch the light on their hard, reflective surface and show as brilliant spots of light on the dark cloth. Buttons and feathers and braid can be expensive. It is worth considering carefully, when it is necessary to save on the budget, that details of braid may be lost on the audience. Seam tape or bias binding may do the job just as well for much less money.

Haberdashery

Haberdashery is the thread and tape, fastenings and bindings that are used in dressmaking; all the invisible nuts and bolts that are used in the construction of a costume. They may be invisible, but they are essential and expensive. Do not be tempted to believe that, when you have paid for the fabric, trimmings and accessories of a costume, you have paid for the whole thing. It is astonishing how much can be spent on thread, elastic and hooks and eyes; it sometimes comes to as much as the cloth of the costume. Cheap thread is a false economy and will infuriate the maker as it knots and snaps on the machine. However, as with any other supplies, there are bargains to be found if you are careful.

Shoes

There are suppliers of period shoes and boots who sell designs suitable for different eras and will adapt their stock shoes to the designs, fabric and colours you choose. Dancewear specialists sell the sort of shoes that can be useful and are less expensive than period-shoe makers. Footwear sold for the many different disciplines of martial arts can provide some interesting and useful styles, which can be adapted and decorated.

Try to find an imaginative cobbler who is interested in adapting shoes to your designs. He may be able to turn a shoe into a lace-up boot or alter it to allow space for a wolf's claws to stick out of the end. It takes a particular interest and imagination as well as skill to solve these sort of problems, and you will probably have to put up with several people treating you as if you were deranged before you find someone who understands what you want. When you find them, stick to them like glue because they are a rare breed.

Hosiery

Dancewear shops sell tights for men as well as women. Party shops sell striped and patterned stockings and so do some markets that cater to an ethnic mix of shoppers. Seamed stockings can be bought in large department stores and sex shops. The denier may be too fine for the purpose, in which case you may have to use them over a pair of ordinary women's tights. You may find thick stockings and tights in very old-fashioned drapery shops in towns where there is a large elderly population. The thick Lycra tights worn by ballet dancers can be dyed from their pink or white to a

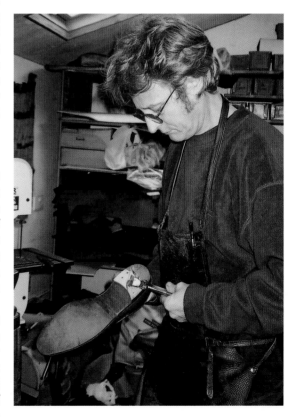

An interested and imaginative shoemaker can alter shoes to your design.

more homely beige shade. Support hose are thicker than usual tights.

Men's knee socks and stockings for wearing with breeches or plus fours can be found in fishing or shooting shops or specialists that supply clerical and ecclesiastical garb. A few bishops, for instance, still wear purple socks and you can also find knee-length fine-knit black socks and all sorts of other goodies through these venerable portals. School suppliers, particularly those that supply the more eccentric and expensive school uniforms, sell long grey socks and other clothes that have long gone out of fashion.

Antique Clothes

There are shops that specialize in period clothes, although of course you can rarely find anything more than a hundred years old that has any chance of standing up to the rigors of theatrical life. Women of earlier times did not use anti-perspirant, so most dresses and blouses have rotted under the arms. Men's clothes, being heavier and worn over cotton shirts, have lasted better, although many actors of today, even when very slim, have a more athletic build than men of a hundred years ago.

Hats

There are milliners who will make hats to your design. Shops that supply materials and equipment to milliners also sell hat shapes that can be steamed and shaped, as well as all the haberdashery, net, veiling, feathers, glues and stiffenings. It is best to go and look around their stock if you are not familiar with the ins and outs of millinery; they are full of items that are useful to costumiers.

Specialists

Suppliers that specialize in stage, film and dance costume can be found through their advertisements in trade paper and journals. The internet will provide further information if you narrow down the field enough; if you search under 'horse riding' for outfits it may take hours to find something of interest, but if you search under 'side-saddle riding habits', you should find what you need fairly quickly.

SHOPPING FOR FABRIC

Quantities

You might be able to cut a pair of trousers for a thin man out of one width of material; the same sort of trousers for a man the same height, but much fatter, may take twice the length, as you will not be able to cut wide enough trousers from a single width. Allow plenty for turnings and extras such as collars and pocket flaps. If you have doubts about your ability to gauge how much fabric to buy, look at a modern dressmaking pattern of a style that is roughly similar, and use that as a guide. You should be able to guess whether you will need to allow an extra length for a fuller skirt or wide coat-tails.

You may have to buy extra cloth if the design is large and can only be used in one direction. Imagine a cloth with a pattern of large roses set apart on a plain background. You would want to place the pattern pieces so that the roses showed to advantage and not so that one side of the bodice had a rose over the bosom and the other side half a rose concealed in the side seam. Even when you lay the whole cloth out and jig-saw the pieces around to fit the cloth in the most economical way, there will be quite a lot of waste. Big checks or wide stripes use extra cloth because the pattern will have to be matched on the seams; stripes that join clumsily at the seams will look even worse from a distance than they do in the workroom.

The nap of the cloth is another factor to take into consideration. If you stroke a piece of velvet or corduroy downwards, it will feel smooth and silky. If you stroke it upwards it will feel rough; it's like stroking the cat the wrong way. This effect is called the nap. If you look at two pieces of the same cloth with the nap going in opposite directions they will look as if they are different colours; the light is reflected by the surface of the cloth in different ways and can change its appearance dramatically. This means that you cannot turn pattern pieces upside-down to fit more economically on the cloth. You must allow more cloth so that you can cut all the pattern pieces in the same direction.

A pattern that requires the fabric to be used on the cross, or the bias, is always an extravagant

Laying out the pattern to make the best use of the cloth.

eater-up of cloth. The fabric drapes and flows particularly well when cut on the bias and tends to mould to the body with a facility that makes the extravagance worthwhile. The bias-cut dresses of the 1930s that cling and flutter as they move would be halved in their effect if cut straight up and down the grain of the cloth.

Take the designs with you when shopping. Every time you buy a length of cloth, cut a small sample from it and keep it with the design. It will be a running record of the fabrics and colours of each project and will help you make decisions when you are buying the cloth for a production at many different sources. It is impossible to remember the colours and fabrics without a reminder, and all the other bits and bobs will also have to be matched. The braid and buttons and belts and shoes will all become part of a single actor's costume, so do not leave home without your sheaf of drawings (or photocopies of drawings). Carry a stapler with you, too, particularly if you are shopping at lots of different shops, so that you can attach the sample with the price to the business card of the supplier.

Where to Find Fabric

As well as the more regular shops and department stores, you can try market stalls and ethnic shops, and shops that specialize in end-of-lines and unusual cloth. Their products may be perfect for you and they should be relatively cheap, particularly if they are unsuitable for dressmaking. There is also a wealth of bargains to be had in fire- or flood-damaged stock, or in fabric that has emerged from the factory with flaws, or has faded edges where the light has bleached them out in the shop window. All these disasters for the seller are happy advantages to the costume shopper who is trying to make the best of a tight budget. Flaws in cloth, unless they have created a dramatic colour change or a very noticeable mistake in the weave, will not be visible to the audience. Damage can be cut round and the eccentricity that led to the end-of-line bargain staying on the retailer's shelf may endear it to the costume maker's heart.

You have to be imaginative and to see the possibilities. You may see a length of lightweight viscose that matches your design to perfection but is not heavy enough – the design suggests thick wool. You could decide that the design and colour are such lucky matches that it would be worth backing the thin cloth with a thicker fabric to achieve the weight. There are all sorts of tricks you can play because the audience cannot get close enough to feel the fabric and the stage lights will make everything look its best. You can, of course, dye plain cloth but you can also dye a patterned

65

A skirt hem with a painted border.

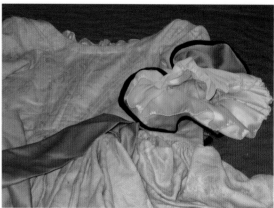

A bodice decorated with binding and frills and ribbons made of remnants.

fabric to accentuate or fade out a pattern. You can exaggerate, alter or add to a pattern with fabric paints. You can chop up a chair cover and make it into a bodice if the colour happens to suit your purpose. There is nothing to stop you using cloth inside-out if you prefer the wrong side, or cutting off a selvedge and reapplying it on another edge like braid.

There are no rules – except those of practicality. Making costumes for the theatre is not like dressmaking and there are all sorts of dodges that would make a very poor showing in the world of fashion, but solve endless costume problems. They are never real clothes, even at their most naturalistic, any more than an actor playing Jack the Ripper is a real villain.

SHOPPING FOR TRIMMINGS

There are shops that specialize in braid, buttons, tassels and ribbon. Department stores with a good haberdashery section may have an excellent range, although some may be stocked in the upholstery rather than the dressmaking department. Work out, with reference to the design, how many yards of trimming you need and how many buttons, and buy just a little too much or too many. You may need matching ribbon to trim a hat, a spare button is always useful if the design is hard to match, and

braid that is to be sewn on a washable garment may shrink. It may horrify you when you realize how easy it is to spend money on braid and buttons. It can cost as much as or more than the cloth and it is just as important that it should look right. Again, it is useful to cut small samples to add to your folder.

Braid on a Budget

It is always cheaper to buy a whole roll of braid than to buy by the metre and some of the items suggested here are in such common use in the Wardrobe that it is worth keeping a supply at hand – if you have enough money to support the initial outlay. Always imagine the effect the audience will see when you are buying braid – half-close your eyes and look from a distance if you find it hard to guess how much of the detail will cross the footlights to the audience.

Tape
Everyday black or white tape is easy to track down in several widths. It is always cheaper to order a whole roll, which is usually between 25 and 50m (30–55yds). The decorative finishes and complicated weave that make braid expensive are often invisible on stage, so you are paying for something the audience will never see. You might put four rows of narrow black tape round the hem

of the sleeves and skirt of a Victorian dress, or outline a man's jacket with a sporty band sewn close to the edge of jacket hems, sleeves and lapels. A wider tape, sewn over a ridge created by sewing the tape bridged over a cord, could be rubbed with gold to edge a cloak or crown. A gathering thread along the top edge of the widest white tape will create a finished frill, or a white flower, if a glob of paint or a bead is set in the centre. Seam tape comes in a wide range of colours and has a slightly glossy finish, which looks good onstage. There are all sorts of other possibilities, such as petersham and grosgrain waist banding, all of which are very much cheaper than braid and can be dressed up adding a narrow Russia braid to give extra interest to a simple edging.

Bias Binding

Bias binding has the great advantage of working well in curves. It is cut in strips on the bias (diagonal to the weave) of cloth and sold folded over at each side for easy application. You can make it yourself, if you have the time and patience, from bias strips. There is a small gadget called a bias tape maker, which helps with the folding and pressing, but it is still a bit of a fiddle.

Bias can be bought in widths ranging from 13mm (about half an inch) to 50mm (2in), in a huge range of colours and in a silky as well as a plain cotton finish. Occasionally, you can find bias binding patterned with checks, flowers or stripe.

The easiest way to use bias binding as decoration is to sew one edge very close to the edge of the fold. Press it with steam to set it in the place where you want it to lie, and then stitch the other edge as close to the fold as you can manage. If you are creating a design with very tight curves you may have to run a gathering line of stitches along the inside curve before you press and sew it on to the costume.

Ribbon

Ribbon can be a real drain on the budget, particularly when it is wide or double-sided. You might get away with decorating a very brash hat, perhaps for a pantomime character, with the papery ribbon that is used for gift wrapping, but it will never pass as the real thing. It can be quite quick, particularly if working with a cloth that you can rip across the width in a straight line, to make your own ribbons; finish the torn edges with a zigzag machine edging. This will create a ribbon that, with its slightly furry edge, will have a period look to it. It uses up more time than buying the real thing, but the effect is often better and the choice of cloth is huge. It is noticeable if ribbons and bows are skimpy so at least you can feel that your budget-saving efforts will make a considerable difference to the audience.

Cord and Tassels

Narrow cord is readily found in many colours at an affordable price but thicker cord and tassels can be expensive. Cotton piping cord is only made in white or cream, but it can be dyed to any colour you want. Thinner cords can be plaited to make thick ones and you can create a cord out of wool or string by twisting it tightly, bending it over at the midway point and encouraging it to twiddle itself round itself. Jersey fabric, panne velvet and even old T-shirts, when cut in narrow strips across the width of the cloth, will often roll up when tugged gently, and create a perfect tube, with no need for any stitching. This can be used as a thick cord to make tassels or plaits.

Buttons

Buttons vary enormously in terms of price and quality. They are an extremely practical type of fastening for stage costumes as they are reliable, and if one drops off the others will carry on doing the job. One added advantage is that it looks perfectly natural for an actor to do up a button on stage, whereas press studs, hooks and eyes or Velcro all require two hands and a downward glance. Buttons have a decorative function as well as a practical one. A line of closely spaced buttons down the front of a bodice may be all the decoration it needs. Think of a plain dark blue man's jacket with matt, dark buttons; replacing the plain buttons with silver ones, and perhaps adding epaulettes with another button, will quickly transform it from a civilian garment to a uniform.

It is useful to keep a stock of buttons, and they are much cheaper in quantity than when sold singly. Make sure when you choose buttons that you imagine them onstage – colour and the way they react to the light are more important factors than quality. Some buttons can be dyed using ordinary commercial dye; they can also be painted or sprayed with colour or a metallic finish. Car spray-paint comes in all colours and sticks to most surfaces.

Feathers

Feathers can be bought from haberdashers and craft shops, begged from butchers and found in the countryside. Pale grey and white feathers can be dyed and cut to different shapes. It may be necessary to stiffen the quill with wire to make it behave as you want it to.

BARGAIN SHOPPING

Car-boot, garage and jumble sales have to be the staple shopping grounds for a production with a very low budget, and the most exciting possibilities can lie hidden in the most dispiriting-looking stall. It takes practice to recognize these possibilities, and to know how much to pay for them. Unless the proceeds are for charity, it is quite reasonable, and indeed expected, to offer a price that may be lower than the stallholder suggests.

The first rule is to know what you are looking for and not to be distracted from your costume search. The second rule is to have enough cash in small change; few stallholders will take cards or cheques and there are times when it is impossible to change a twenty- or even a ten-pound note. The third rule is to have plenty of bags, plenty of optimism and an ability to see the potential in an unlikely purchase.

Charity-shop shopping takes place in a more organized environment, where everything is sorted and priced. Some will take credit cards and most will take cheques. There are tills and receipts. You can see the stock and how much it costs and the prices, as the profits go to various charities, are not negotiable. Charity shops vary in price and content. A charity shop in a smart area is likely to have smarter clothes and be more expensive than one in a less privileged neighbourhood. You are more likely to find country clothes in the country shops and city clothes in towns.

Second-hand shopping for contemporary plays is fairly straightforward. It is a matter of finding something that looks right, sits well within the design brief to which you are working, and will fit the actor, or could be altered to fit the actor who is going to wear it. Buying modern clothes for period productions is a different skill and it helps if you have experience of altering and re-cutting clothes. It is essential that you have a clear picture in your mind of the sort of clothes people were wearing in the time of the play you are dressing. You will need to do a bit of homework before you shop to make sure you can picture the shape of an appropriate skirt, the lapels of a jacket, the style of ties and shoes and blouses that you will need to recognize on the stalls and rails.

Jackets Look at the shape of the collar. Can you add another button and buttonhole to make it fasten higher? Could you round the bottom front corners or shorten it? Could you make it more fitted at the waist or alter its appearance with braid? Could you use the cloth from matching suit trousers to make major alterations to the sleeves or the collar? Is it possible to re-cut the shape of a jacket if you bind the edge? A man's jacket turned inside-out and with the lining ripped out provides a wealth of different colours and fabrics in the linings, interlinings and stiffening that are usually invisible as they are neatly concealed by the lining.

Men's trousers and suits Look for trousers of an old-fashioned cut where the length from crotch to waist is longer than that of modern trousers. Any trousers that have braces buttons and many with button flies will have this extra length. The cloth from the trousers of a suit can be cut into tails and added to the re-cut jacket to give the impression of a nineteenth-century tailcoat. Formal clothes, such as dinner suits (black jacket with silk lapels and trousers with a braided stripe down the side), tails (very formal 'monkey jacket', cut high in the front and with two tails at the back) or morning suits (the suit worn at formal weddings, with a grey or black coat with a swallow tail curved from the front) are often sold in excellent condition, as people wear them so seldom. Trousers can be cut off into breeches and the cloth from the lower leg used to make the knee bands. There is not much that can be done to widen trouser legs but they can be narrowed, shortened or lengthened if there is a hem or turn-ups. False turn-ups can be created by stitching in a tuck to create the lines of highlight and shadow that will look like a turn-up onstage.

Waistcoats Waistcoats are always useful. All the difficult work – pockets and buttonholes – has been done for you and it is a simple matter to take up the shoulders to give a higher fastening at the front, or to straighten it at the bottom if you need to get rid of the points.

Shirts Look for double cuffs and good-quality cotton and a fullness of cut, perhaps with gathers or pleats on a yoke, if you are looking for a pre-1950-style shirt. Collars are the most obvious indicator of period and can be altered by cutting a new one from the tail of the shirt, which the audience will never see. A collar can be cut off to a new shape and zigzagged round with a close stitch, or bound with bias. A modern shirt collar, if turned up and re-cut, can look acceptably old-fashioned when helped by an appropriate cravat. Look out for thicker shirts, perhaps with stripes, for the workers in your performance; the collars can be re-made into a band and finished with a neckerchief.

Blouses Shoulders can be re-cut and collars altered. Completely new sleeves can be made if there is a skirt of the same cloth to cut from, or sleeves can be shortened or removed completely. You can cut a puff sleeve from a long sleeve by using the length as the width. Blouses can be made more fitted by putting darts in the body.

Sweaters Sweaters can be altered without the need for unpicking and re-knitting. Choose the right colour and texture, and zigzag or tape seams before you cut them, or the whole garment will begin to

unravel. Care must be taken to finish all cut edges with several lines of stitching.

Dresses You can chop dresses in half and use just the top or just the bottom. If you use the top, the skirt can become sleeves or peplum, new cuffs or different collar; if you use the skirt, the top can be chopped up to make waistband, pockets or perhaps a headscarf. Modern dresses are not much use for any costume before the 1940s as they will be too short, unless you are dressing the mid-1920s, or come across an evening dress or a 1970s dress with an ankle-length hem. However, you can alter shoulders and collars and details of trimmings.

Skirts The same problem of length exists but many skirts have quite a lot of cloth in them, which can be used to make other things.

Coats Male and female coats can be re-cut into jackets. A lightweight formal man's overcoat can be converted into a pretty convincing frock coat or longer jacket. A female overcoat might become a riding coat or an outdoor jacket from an earlier period.

A woman's cardigan is transformed into a man's V-necked sweater.

An impression of the early 1940s is created with modern second-hand clothes, and using the sweater illustrated on the previous page. Photo: Nik Mackey

Shoes When buying second-hand shoes, the first thing to check is their condition. If they are down-at-heel or well worn, reject them, even if they are perfect period shoes. It is not reasonable to ask actors to wear footwear that wear and tear has shaped to other feet. However, it is often possible to buy shoes that have scarcely been worn and there is a surprising amount you can do, even if you are not a cobbler, to alter shoes, particularly if they are made of leather. Leather can be cut with scissors and sewn on an ordinary sewing machine. You can buy special machine needles and hand-sewing needles that make the job easier. The tops of shoes can be re-cut or made to lace up in a different way so that the tongue covers the laces. Bows or buckles or rosettes can be attached. Leather takes kindly to dye, paint and glue.

Accessories Bags, ties, scarves, hats, stockings and handkerchiefs, jewellery and belts – they will all be there, hidden amongst the mass of useless junk. All you have to do is find them and recognize that they are useful.

Haberdashery It is surprising how often rolls of tape and elastic and bias bindings appear on the stalls at a fraction of the cost in a department store, as well as dyes, lace and ribbon. Be wary when buying thread. Make sure it is a brand you know; it is soul-destroying to use poor-quality thread that knots and snaps and, although it can be expensive, it pays to buy the best. Old tablecloths and teacloths may be in threadbare, stained condition, but may be bordered with lace perfect for a cavalier collar or an Edwardian blouse. Lace is surprisingly tough and you can usually boil it up or wash it in the machine on a hot wash, and it will iron as smooth as new. Use a muslin bag if you are washing it in the machine, or you may have to spend hours untangling it.

Cloth A grubby, faded pair of curtains can have new life as Andrew Aguecheek's doublet or Hedda Gabler's skirt. Rip out linings, curtain tape and hems, put it through the washing machine and see what you end up with; remember, it may be the wrong side of the cloth that attracts you. Velvet and silk curtains often fade in vague-edged stripes, which, with thoughtful cutting, can give a costume a beautiful time-worn look that would be hard to reproduce with bleach and dye. Pure cotton, perhaps a set of old sheets, is always useful for linings, if nothing else. You may be the only person to recognize the value of a length of silk, which will dye to any colour you like.

All this bargain shopping takes skill and practice. You need to know that it will take you less time to adapt a garment than to make it from scratch. Long, straight seams and darts are no problem. It is the work of a few moments to take in a side seam. A long hem will take minutes once you have mastered the hemstitch on your machine. The things that take the time are buttonholes and facings, collars and lapels, making pockets and trouser flies and fastenings generally. Unpicking will be quicker with practice, as you become more confident about which cloth will stand the strain of you ripping the seam apart, and which seams will have to be taken apart with delicacy and care. If you are taking things in and have cloth to spare in the turnings, you will often be able to use the extra-quick method of cutting a seam apart rather than unpicking it.

You really need to enjoy the bargain hunting, as it can be chilly and dispiriting. It can also be exciting and addictive and you will find that you become better and quicker at scanning a stall and spotting treasures. Many people interested in costume also enjoy discovering it in an unlikely place. Once you get your eye in and become good at recognizing period fabrics and cut, you can find the most beautiful and perfect clothes, accessories and cloth in the jumble of a stall.

The random heaps of clothes and objects give the designer an added and more ephemeral benefit in creating surprising combinations of textures, colours and shapes. You will not see such combinations in the more considered arrangement of a shop, and they can provide an inspiration to the imagination and kick-start a fresh approach to your designs.

HIRING

There can be a big difference in cost, quality and reliability between hire firms. The more expensive ones, which cater for films and television as well as theatre, have a huge range of costumes and expert staff who can advise you on the correct clothes and accessories for different periods, and will sometimes make costumes to your designs. The smaller firms will have a less extensive range and you may have to be more adaptable in your ideas to create the set of costumes you have imagined. In all cases, it is best to choose the clothes yourself.

Some hire firms have a measurement form they ask you to fill in in advance, then select a rail of costumes for you to choose from. Others invite you to choose from the racks yourself, selecting style and size until you have assembled the full set of costumes. In all cases, you will need a set of measurements for each actor. It is a good idea to select the costumes as early as you can, particularly for a production around Christmas time, a hire firm's busiest period, or if you need something out of the ordinary. The costumes can be reserved for your production and the hire charge will not begin until they are delivered.

It can be more economical to hire, rather than make, when the costumes will only be needed for a few consecutive nights. It can become a very expensive option when the play is running for longer, or the performances are spread out over a long tour, as a weekly charge will be made on each costume. Hired costumes may have to be altered, and the charges dictate that they should arrive as late as is practicable. Be prepared to have to sit up late altering and adapting if the costumes do not arrive until the tech. rehearsal, or, worse still, before the dress rehearsal.

6 CUTTING

Cutting is perhaps the most frightening part of costume-making, particularly for the inexperienced maker. It is easy to fear that your mistakes will be fatal to the costume and there is something daunting about slicing your way into an untouched length of velvet. You will have seen costumes on films and in the theatre and think it impossible that yours could be as good. The only comfort is that it gets easier each time you do it, and few mistakes are truly irrevocable.

There are all sorts of tricks to help the inexperienced cutter. The most valuable advice is keep calm, concentrate, do not cut when you are tired or likely to be distracted, and remember that the way other people do it is not necessarily the best way. This chapter will be most useful to people who are inexperienced in cutting costumes and do not have convenient equipment. It assumes that you have had some experience of using a commercial pattern for a contemporary garment. If you have never made anything from a pattern, buy an easy one (the pattern books in haberdashery departments or fabric shops are graded with the degree of difficulty), and make it, following the step-by-step instructions exactly. This will teach you how a pattern works, why you need the markings and notches, and, once you have made up the garment, you can see how you could have made the legs wider, the sleeves fuller, or allowed for a pleat in the back.

If you look at some of the more complicated books of period costume patterns, you may feel you are not up to the job. They reproduce the exact way that the genuine costumes found in museums and collections were made, and most of them look very complicated indeed. They can be enlarged and reproduced exactly, and there is no doubt that costumes made by expert makers in this way can look absolutely wonderful, giving a genuine feeling of the past. These instructions are much easier to follow once you have bodged your way through a few costumes and are beginning to understand the best way to achieve the effects you want.

It helps if you have had some pattern-cutting training. It helps even more if you can work with someone more experienced than you, who will alert you to mistakes before they happen. The more experience you have of any sort of cutting and making, the easier you will find it to get started. But even the most expert cutting and perfect construction can be ruined if an actress strides along as if she were wearing jeans and trainers and uses her fan like a tennis racket, and few of the audience will be conscious of those perfect period seams.

PATTERNS

Until you have had quite a lot of practice you will want to use a pattern of some kind. This can be an old garment cut apart at the seams and pressed flat, a shape chalked directly on to the cloth, or a paper pattern. You may have scaled up the pattern on to paper from a book on the cut of historical costumes. You may have tracked down a modern commercial pattern of a period costume from information supplied by a website devoted to clubs that re-enact the Civil War or the Wars of the Roses. You may be using a commercial modern pattern and altering it to suit the design – after all,

Deciding on the Shape

The design may show the placing of the seams and details such as pockets and cuffs. Alternatively, it may give a general idea, leaving the details up to the cutter to decide. Most periods have a particular way of placing seams, which show off to advantage the fashionable figure of the time. The curved back seams of a Victorian bodice accentuate a tiny waist. Darts that shape the mid-twentieth-century blouse to the waist will tend to run down to the waistline about half-way between the centre-back and the side seam. On the Victorian bodice, the back will be cut in separate pieces and the shaping will run from the armhole to a few centimetres either side of the centre-back. The lack of bust darts on 1920s dresses and bust darts on 1950s dresses encourage the fashionable bosom of each era, and are rarely used at all in the Lycra tops of today. It is such details, getting the seams the right shape and in the right place, that make a costume convincing.

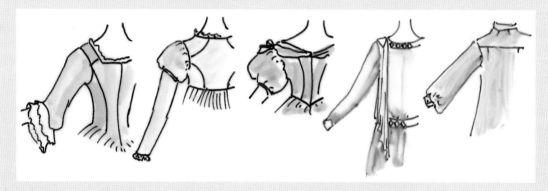

The way seams are placed at the back of a costume accentuates the fashionable figure of the era.

there is not that much difference between the business suit of today and the lounge suit of 1930 that cannot be demonstrated by quite minor alterations. Or you may be using one of the fancy-dress patterns that are sold along with those for modern clothes. Some paper-pattern companies offer a 'Historical' range, and these are more convincing than the fancy-dress patterns.

Taking a Pattern from an Existing Garment

Cut the garment in half and use one half to make the pattern and keep its mirror image as an example of how to make it up. (If the garment is asymmetrical you cannot, of course, keep one mirror image complete as an example and must make clear notes as you go.) Cut the half you are using as a pattern into its component parts through the seams; unpick it if you have time, marking matching points with notches or pencil marks. Press the pieces flat. Remember to add seam allowances when you cut.

You can also take a pattern from a garment without destroying it. The pieces of simple garments can be copied by laying flat the different sections on paper and drawing round the seams. Complicated clothes can be copied more easily using a lightweight cloth to make the pattern, which you can turn and pin round the complex curves of each section, cutting out as you go. With all symmetrical garments you need only cut the pattern for one half as the other will mirror it.

Using Patterns in Books

You can buy books that print scaled-down but

exact reproductions of historic costume, taken from actual garments of the era. The bodies that wore them, and the demands that were made on them, will have been very different from those of today. Scale the patterns up to human proportions and measure the finished size. It is likely that you will have to make alterations in this size to fit the modern body, both in the breadth and the height, but the shaping produced by the seams, and the relative position of the seams on the body, can remain the same. Make a garment in miniature from one of these patterns if you are right at the beginning of making period costumes. You can scale the pattern up slightly on a photocopier, which is quick and easy, then cut your little garment of scrap material and sew it up. It will demonstrate to you exactly how the pattern works without wasting cloth, and should give you confidence to make a full-size version.

Costume-making books with patterns specific-ally designed for stage costume will be adapted to modern bodies and are easier to use, if not as accurate in historical terms. They are usually arranged by period and you may find that studying the examples enables you to create patterns of your own. Find the example that is closest to the design you have to cut, and adapt it to fit the picture. These patterns tend to be simpler than the reproductions of genuine historical patterns and are perhaps easier, although not as exciting, for a beginner to follow.

Fancy-Dress Patterns

Examples of these can be found in the pattern books in fabric and haberdashery shops and via the internet. They can be a godsend to someone who has had no experience of costume-making and finds themselves in the position of having to cut a period dress or suit. They are, however, created for fancy dress and party wear, which is not the same as theatre wear. Use them with caution and approach them with a critical eye. For example, you may find a Victorian fancy-dress costume an unconvincing version of the dresses you have studied in your research of the period. It will probably be too lightweight and loose; it may look as if the body is uncorseted and it may be braided

and buttoned in a way that owes more to modern fashion than to the past.

You will find similar patterns for corsets, men's suits and military uniforms. They will provide a manageable starting point for the untrained cutter and, with careful fitting and braiding, and a fabric that looks appropriate to the class and period of the character, can make a good costume.

Modern Commercial Patterns

There is a huge variety of modern patterns available, and they can be most useful, from something as simple as pull-on shorts and a T-shirt to a formal three-piece suit with shirt and tie. There will be examples of hats, bags, ties and underwear, and they will be all scaled to different sizes. They always have a list of measurements, which you can compare with those of the actor who is going to wear the costume. They do tend to be cut rather generously in width, and the crotch to waist seam may be rather short for stage trousers and will have to be lengthened.

These patterns can form the basis for a design, which you can then vary. You may find it useful to use the shoulder and armhole as it is on the pattern and re-cut the neckline to a different shape, or you could use a modern shirt pattern to create a full-sleeved romantic shirt by increasing the width of the top of the sleeve and cutting a different collar.

The Toile

A toile is a mock-up of a garment in a cheap cloth that may be wasted. The toile is cut, pinned or tacked together, fitted on the actor, then taken apart and used as a pattern. It is a much less risky way of doing things if you are not confident of getting it right first time. It also means you can jig-saw the pieces accurately on the cloth, which can be essential if you have a limited amount of fabric or want the design of the fabric to end up carefully placed on the finished garment. Toiles can be made of muslin, cotton, calico, old sheets, or any other fabric of a suitable weight. They can also become the lining of the finished garment. In this case the cloth will not be wasted and must be pre-shrunk before cutting.

Sometimes a length of fabric is draped and twisted round the model or dummy with the designer cutting as he drapes. The dress must be pinned or tacked securely before it is taken off the dummy or model. It is only too easy for the designer to create marvellous swags and draping that seem to disappear and make no sense to the maker who has to create a finished garment from the toile.

More structured shapes, perhaps a close-fitting bodice or corset, are cut accurately to the measurements. The bodice, cut in calico or strong cotton, is pinned firmly at the seams and fitted on the actress. The pins, on the outside of the garment, are moved until the shape fits like a second skin and the armholes, neckline and waistline are adjusted to suit the actress's body. This shape is then used as a pattern to cut the bodice from the real cloth.

CUTTING THE CLOTH

Preparation

You will need a flat surface, large enough to lay out the cloth; you may have to use the floor for larger items. Avoid working on carpet, because pins get stuck in it, cloth will not slide on it and it can take a long time to clean up all the little threads afterwards. The measurements of the actor, the design, scissors, tape measure, metre/yard rule, and tailor's chalk or pencil are pretty well essential (although a long batten can take the place of the rule for long straight-line marking). There are all

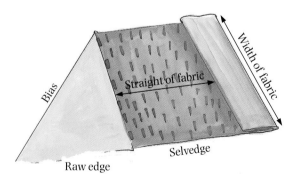

Cloth vocabulary.

sorts of curved templates you can buy, but you can use any rounded shapes to draw curves. A weight or two can be very useful when you are working with slippery cloth on a slippery table. Keep a rubbish bin close by and a separate box or basket for scraps you want to keep, so that the two do not get muddled.

The fabric you are cutting should be ironed and pre-shrunk by washing and steam ironing before you cut it. If there is a possibility of the cloth being tumble-dried at some time in its future life, tumble it dry before you start. The tumble drier can shrink cloth even more than the washing machine.

Laying Out the Cloth

The straight or the length of the cloth is the length of the cloth that you buy measured along the selvedge, which is the finished edge that runs down both sides of the cloth. The width of the cloth is from selvedge to selvedge. Fold the straight edge of the cloth in a triangle so that it aligns with the selvedge; the fold is the bias of the cloth. Most cloth hangs best on the straight and most patterns repeat down the straight. The bias is slightly elastic and stretches more than either the straight or the width. Cloth woven with even a small proportion of stretchy fibre, such as Lycra or Elastane, hangs well in any direction. The dressmaking rule that demands most garments are cut with the straight grain of the cloth running up and down the garment is often broken with theatre costumes, where the only rule is that they should look right and be practical. It can be convenient and time-saving, despite being against all dressmaking rules, to cut a very full skirt using the selvedge as the hem – why not, if it works? Keep remembering that you do not have to be able to cut and sew perfectly to make theatre costumes.

You may want to create a straight edge at the top of the fabric. Some cloth will tear in a straight line – it is impossible to tell which until you try, but it is the quickest way to get a straight edge. Some designs allow you to cut across, using the flowers or stripes as a guide. On some fabric you can draw out one thread to give a clear line across the width. Alternatively, you can draw a line at right-angles to the selvedge with a long ruler or batten.

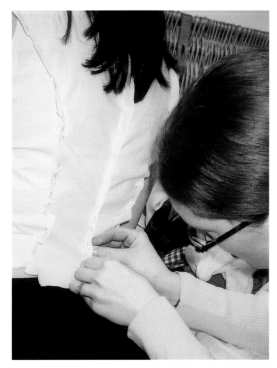

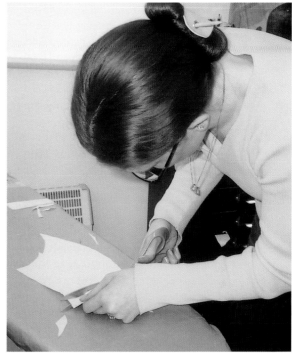

*ABOVE LEFT: **Fitting the toile to the body.***

*ABOVE RIGHT: **Adjusting the toile pattern after fitting.***

*RIGHT: **Cutting the cloth from the fitted pattern.***

Work with the cloth folded right sides together so that you are cutting, for instance, a left front and a right front in mirror image. If the cloth has stripes or checks that are bold enough to be noticed onstage, make sure it is lined up so that it matches; remember to line it up on the seam and not at the edge of the seam allowance. When using a paper or cloth pattern, use as few pins as you can to attach it to the cloth; weights are more convenient and disturb the way the cloth is lying less than pins do.

Cutting to Size

Cut more generous seam allowances than are allowed on commercial patterns, which allow 2cm (five-eighths of an inch) as the norm. It can be the saving of a bodice that does not quite fit to have enough seam allowance at the shoulders to let out, so that the whole bodice can slide down the body. Many theatre costumes are re-used by different actors and it is sensible to make them easy to let out and take in. Be particularly generous with the centre-back seam as the energetic movement of actors becomes difficult if the garment is tight across the shoulders. Many actors are gymnasts, acrobats and dancers, and both women and men tend to have broader shoulders and more muscled arms than less active people. Stage clothes have a different lifestyle from street clothes; you would not expect a lady in a formal evening dress to turn a somersault, but an actress might have to night after night, and twice on matinee days.

Do not trust measurements to be exact. Many people assume their waist is where their trousers start and will measure too low, and will have no idea at all where to start and finish a neck-to-waist, or waist-to-knee measurement. It is much easier to take things in than let them out. Straight seams are easier to alter than curved ones.

Chest/bust Allow extra at the side seams and centre-front and centre-back seams. It easier to adjust the measurement at centre-back, front or side than to change the vertical curved seam over the breast or shoulder blades when the pattern has a body where both the front and back are cut in four or more sections.

Waist Allow enough to let out if necessary. Allow extra length in case the nape-to-waist measurement is wrong, which is often the case.

Armholes Do not cut too low or too scooped; you can reshape them on the body at the fitting.

Neckline One of the most common mistakes is to cut necks too wide. This is because it is not easy to guess how small the circle is formed by the circumference of the neck. Put your two forefingers and thumbs round your neck and then look at the circle they form; it helps to put neck measurements into perspective. The neck is lower at the front than at the back. A neckline is easy to re-cut at the fitting before the collar or finishing is attached.

Shoulders Allow plenty of length and a wide seam allowance. It is often necessary to unpin the shoulder seam at a fitting and replace the seam line so that the cloth lies smoothly. It may be necessary to lengthen the whole bodice by dropping it from the shoulder. The extra width at the armhole will enable you to allow more width across the back shoulders. The extra cloth, which can be trimmed after the fitting, leaves you the option of adapting the shape to the actor's body.

Trousers Allow plenty of length from crotch to waist. Allow for the circumference of the thigh to increase when the knee is bent and the calf muscle to expand when flexed. Cut too long if in doubt.

Skirts Allow enough length; when a skirt is worn over a thick petticoat or a crinoline, it uses up extra length. Skirts often hang better with a deep hem. Make sure there is enough room in the hip measurement to allow the actress to sit down. Remember that skirt length seen from below (the front row of the stalls) looks shorter and shows more leg.

Breeches Allow extra length at the front of the knee, which will be needed when the leg is bent, and extra crotch-to-waist height so that the waistband will be hidden under a short waistcoat. The below-knee measurement expands considerably when the knee is bent, so allow for this in the kneeband.

Cloaks Allow plenty of fullness. A circular cloak can be marked out using a piece of string or tape as a compass. Mark slots for the wrists to come through at the fitting, when you will be able to see their natural position.

Pockets It is easier to mark and cut pockets when the garment is flat. If you are unsure of the placing, you will have to wait until the fitting to check it.

Corsets A corset must fit the body very closely so there is little point in leaving generous seam allowances unless you are unsure of your pattern. Laced corsets should be cut a little small in width to allow the laces to do their work in shaping the figure.

Padding Padding is cut double. The inner layer fits the skin and the outer layer is cut more generously to allow for an infilling of wadding or foam.

Collars, facings, and so on It is better to cut these after the first fitting when the size and depth of the neck hole have been adjusted.

Using Scissors

Try to cut a smooth line without jags. It is easier if you keep the lower blade of the scissors on the table all the time and think about the whole slice of the cut from beginning to end, rather than each snip. Cut with confidence, as if you were drawing a line with a pencil. Slice just beyond a corner, as it is difficult to turn the scissors in a right-angle and keep the cloth and the pattern, if you are using one, in position.

Marking

Cut tiny little snips, between 3 and 7mm (⅛ and ¼in) long, depending on the thickness of the fabric, to mark darts at the seams, to mark matching points on seams and to remind you of any other significant points, such as the place a collar joins a lapel, when you come to stitch the garment. These little snips or notches can be single, double or triple. It helps to get into the habit of always using double notches for the back of a garment and single for the front. These tiny snips have the same purpose as the black triangles printed and numbered on commercial patterns. They can save a great deal of pinning and you will know, even when working in a great rush, that if the notches do not match up something is amiss in your work. Markings that need to be made in the main body of a pattern piece, such as the point of a dart, can be done with a pencil dot, a small safety pin, an ordinary pin if you are confident it will not slip out, or a tailor tack, which is a loop of thread hand-sewn into the cloth. You may need to label the cut pieces, particularly if you are cutting several costumes in different sizes out of the same cloth.

Tips and Tricks

Every costume you cut is different unless you are cutting a set of costumes for performers of a similar size. There are many time-saving tricks that will come in useful over and over again, and many more that you will discover for yourself through experience. Here are a few well-tried favourites.

Sleeves A set-in sleeve will be cut with a deeper scoop in the front than the back. Always, always, always mark the back of the armhole of the sleeve piece with a double notch. It is easy to put the sleeve in the wrong armhole and so dull to have to unpick it, particularly when you are tired and decide to put the sleeve in as a last thing before you go home.

Centres Mark centre points of skirts, trousers, sleeveheads, etc, particularly if they are going to be gathered or pleated, with an outward triangle. This will show up through the gathers where a notch would be buried.

Curved hems Curved hems begin and end at right-angles to the side seams. If you do not curve a hemline on a gored or flared skirt, it will sag and you may waste a good deal of fullness and cloth in the cutting.

Darts and pleats Mark the places where you think they might be set with notches while the pattern pieces are still lying paired up on the table. You will then have mirror-image markings and can match the right-side pleat position with the left-hand pleat position without too much measuring.

Smooth cloth Take great care to get each layer of cloth smooth before you cut. A small, hidden crumple in the cloth can cause a serious mistake in your mirror image.

Cutting for gathers A very full skirt can take many lengths of cloth, which may have to be gathered tightly into a small waistline. Mark the centre point of each width of cloth when you cut it and mark the corresponding divisions in the bodice or waistband. This will make it easier to judge if the gathers are being set in equally.

Overlaps You may have to allow overlaps for plackets, fastenings, flies and double-breasted or wrap-around garments. Always mark the centre line when you are cutting, so that you can match the fastening site accurately.

Collars The easiest way to cut a collar of a difficult shape is to wait until the shoulder seams and centre-front and -back seams have been stitched. Cut a very rough shape for a collar out of waste cloth. Put the garment on the actor or a dummy and pin the collar to the neck edge, snipping and trimming where necessary. When the neck edge is as you want it, cut the outer edge of the collar to the design. Mark the centre-back points, and use the best half of the shape you have cut as a pattern for the whole collar.

Adjoining seams When two seams of a garment have to join, such as the front and back of trousers at the side seam, or the underarm seam of a bodice, cut them together, or lay them one on top of the other to check that both the cloth and the notches really do match. Imagine you are making a skirt. It is smooth at the front but gathered to give extra fullness at the back. The slanting, A-line side seams

will be joined but the back will be a much larger piece of fabric than the front. Spread the front pieces over the back, matching the side seams, either cut and notch both together, and cut the under one to match the top one.

Linings Cut linings at the same time as you cut the top cloth, when everything is flat on the table. It is much harder to do it afterwards when the garment is made up. Mark and notch it in the same way as the top cloth. It is not necessary for linings that will not be seen to match in colour, so it is a good way of using scrap fabric.

Cuffs Mark the back of the cuff with a double notch even if it is a straight piece. You will need to distinguish between the right and left cuff to create a right and left sleeve.

Socks and stockings Socks and stockings and even tights can be cut out of jersey-type cloth, the springier and stretchier the better. Iron a sock or stocking so that it is a flat shape and cut round it, allowing for turnings. You may find when you fit it that it will need a dart at the front of the ankle if the cloth is not very stretchy.

Circles There is a formula for working out exact sizes of circles (πr^2), but for the less mathematically adept, the circumference of a circle is approximately six times its radius. Alternatively, take the measurement, say, a head of 56cm (22in) round, curl your tape measure round to meet at the 56cm (22in) point and find something to draw round that is about that size.

Organization Fold up all the pieces you have cut for each costume in one pile, making sure the small pieces, such as collars, cuffs and pocket flaps, are safely tucked inside. Keep all the scraps until after the dress rehearsal.

OPPOSITE: *Peter Duncan as Jim Hawkins and Iain Hathorn as Jim Hawkins, the boy, in* Treasure Island. *Photo: Robbie Jack*

7 MAKING

Note: This chapter assumes you have some experience of basic sewing techniques and have, and can use, a sewing machine that will go forward and backward and do a zigzag stitch. There are a few skills that you really need to master if you are going to make costumes; *see* the 'Test' section (pages 89–90).

USEFUL TECHNIQUES

The examples in this chapter demonstrate a number of ways of working that will be useful in all sorts of costume-making circumstances. Many of them would seem shocking and slip-shod to a dressmaker. None of the techniques is the only or the right way of doing it – they are just suggestions and ways that experience has shown to be quick, easy and efficient. The advice may become obsolete once you have made a few costumes yourself, as you will find your own ways, which suit your particular style.

The headings refer to the technique and not the garment.

Incidentally, costumes, like all clothes, look better if you press each seam before you join it to another one. Ironing and pressing can save pinning and tacking, can shrink or stretch cloth to make it lie flat or bulge, and can alert you to any mistakes before you stitch. Always test the temperature of the iron on a piece of spare fabric before you put it on the real thing. You can dampen cloth by using a steam irons, a damp muslin cloth, or a water spray, or by putting the fabric in a polythene bag with a couple of tablespoons of water for a couple of hours. Many fabrics are more amenable to ironing when damp, but some react badly and mark, shrivel or die.

Making a Tunic

Imagine you are working on a simple tunic with a collar, a slit in front for fastening, set-in sleeves and a slightly flared hem. The pattern for such a

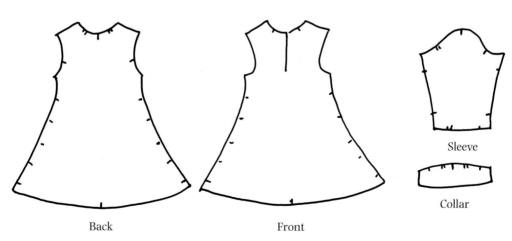

Back   Front

Sleeve

Collar

The tunic.

garment can be found in any commercial pattern book, or you can cut up an old T-shirt and use it as the basis of your pattern.

Zigzagging

If you are going to press the seam open, zigzag raw seam edges before you start. Pull the notches apart slightly as you feed them under the machine foot or mark them with pencil or chalk, as they may vanish within the stitching. Stage clothes are not seen inside-out, so you are finishing the inside for practicality and strength and not for the look of the thing.

Matching Notches

The slanted side seam is on a slight bias, consequently it may stretch as you sew it, and the top layer may stretch more than the bottom. To save having to pin every 10cm (4in) to keep track of the stretch, notch frequently, do not pin, and feed the cloth through the machine, pinching the pairs of notches in the two layers of cloth between finger and thumb as you come to them. It may be necessary to tighten the cloth between your hands behind and in front of the machine foot to keep the notches even, particularly if the two layers are different types of fabric, or one edge is on the straight of the cloth and one edge cut on the bias. Do not stretch too roughly, otherwise the finished seam will ruckle.

Hem on a Gored or Flared Garment

Press the flared seam open. If there is any sort of point at the seam, trim it off to achieve an even hemline. There are a number of ways of proceeding from here:

1. Zigzag round the hem. Press under a narrow hem all the way round. Machine-stitch close to the raw edge, being very careful to keep the same distance from the folded edge. Press again and stitch another line very close to the fold. This is a strong hem and will put up with very rough treatment and quick changes.
2. Press the narrowest turn you can all the way round the hem, turn it up again with a slightly more generous allowance, and

machine-stitch. You can improve the look by pressing again and stitching very close to the lower edge.
3. Zigzag round the edge, then set the machine to a long stitch and machine a line just below the zigzags which will gather in the fullness slightly. Turn up the hem, machine-hem or hand-stitch invisibly and press.
4. Trim the hemline very neat and smooth and zigzag on a small stitch all the way round the hem; this is very quick but only works on cloth that frays hardly at all.
5. Do what your dressmaking handbook suggests for a curved hem.

Setting in Sleeves

Finish the hem, cuff, buttons and decoration of the sleeve before you set it in if possible; it saves turning the whole garment around when you wrestle with braid and hems. Turn the sleeve right side out and check there is a double notch on the back of both sleeves and the back of both armholes. To put in the left sleeve, first check that it really is the left sleeve; if necessary, slip it on your arm, and make sure that the double notches are at the back. Everyone has put a wrong sleeve in or a sleeve in upside-down one tired evening. If there is any epaulette or other decoration, attach it to the armhole before you set in the sleeve.

Turn the garment inside-out. Position the two underarm markings or seams of the sleeve and the armhole, with right sides together, and pin. Work up from the armpit on both sides and position any gathers or pleats near the top, making sure that the top of the sleeve is at the point of the shoulder. Machine-stitch on a long stitch. Turn the garment right side out and have a look. If there are any places where the seam is not as you want it, unpick as little as you can manage and reposition. When you are sure all is well, stitch on a firm stitch, twice round if it is going to take a lot of strain, and trim and zigzag if necessary. Sometimes, costumes are so thick at the shoulder seam, what with pleats and epaulettes and braid and so on, that you will have to use the extra-strong machine needle that is sold for sewing jeans, or a bladed leather needle, to get through the thickness.

Facing used as an asymmetrical decoration on the right side of the garment.

Finishing Slits, Plackets, Etc

Trim the edges of the slit and zigzag with a close stitch, or bind with binding or a strip of fabric. This can be a narrow binding, or a wider one, which you can fold over on one side and use for buttons and buttonholes, or press studs.

Alternatively, sew the shoulder seams of the garment but not the side seams. Cut an echo of the neckline, including the slit, using the garment as a pattern. Cut notches round the neck to help you line it up when you sew. Cut a shape big enough to act as a facing; it can be an elaborate shape in a contrasting colour and can be sewn either as a concealed facing or to show as a decorative feature on the right side. This method will have no overlap unless you pleat it at the bottom of the suit and is excellent for a lace-up fastening on a period shirt or tunic. You can finish the whole neck as well as the slit with the facing if your design does not need a collar, or leave the neck edge to be finished by the attachment of the collar.

A dressmaking handbook will demonstrate more conventional methods.

Collars

All collars Mark the centre-back neck of garment and collar. Mark the place where the collar starts on the opening of the garment (this is particularly important when the finished garment will have lapels). Be meticulous about matching notches and keeping turnings even. Trim off the corners, which would make bulky lumps inside the collar when you turn it right side out. Snip or cut little triangles in any curves with care.

Be a bit finicky with the whole process and press each stage as you go along; collars always show and quite small mistakes are noticeable.

Turn-over collars These collars usually come in two pieces, the under and over collar. On fine cloth they may be exactly the same. On thicker fabric the over collar will be slightly larger than the overlap, to encourage it to fold over. When attaching the collar to the garment, remember to think whether the fastening will overlap (in which case, the collar must be set in a little from the neck edge so that the opening ends up dead centre), or whether it meets as in a laced-up neck (when it must continue to the edge of the opening).

Mandarin and other stand-up collars Decide before you start if the collar will meet in the centre or will overlap, and attach it accordingly. The collar will need an inner stiffening to stand up straight if the cloth is floppy. If it is a transparent fabric, as on the high lace collar of an Edwardian blouse, stiffen it with the lightest bone at the centre-back neck and under the front fastening if you have to. You can buy very thin wavy wire stiffeners for the purpose, but they are hard to find. Alternatively, use the collar stiffeners from a man's shirt or cut little strips out of a supple plastic container like a washing-up liquid bottle.

Cuffs

The most commonplace error is to make the fastening of the cuffs identical instead of mirror image. Although this mistake will not usually be noticed by the audience, it can slow down a quick change, so take care and check as you go along. Attach the underside of the cuff first, press the topside of the cuff in place over the raw edges with a hem turn-in, so that it looks as you want it, and finish with a row of machine topstitching near the edge of the hem. Always make sure the cuff is not too tight. There are many movements when the cuff has to be big enough to slide up the arm to allow for a bended elbow or an upward stretch. When the sleeve going into the cuff is very full, position the greatest bulk of the gathers to fall over the elbow. On a very full sleeve, the back of the sleeve should be cut longer than the front, otherwise the finished sleeve will fall over the hand and may hide the actor's gestures.

Making Trousers

Imagine a pair of trousers with a front fastening and two side pockets.

Flies

The opening will have to be faced or strengthened to support the fastenings. Facings can be cut at the same time as the trousers. Notch the centre-front at the waist. Double-stitch the front crotch seam. Fold and press the fly opening so that it looks right, making sure the fold corresponds with the centre-front notches. Do not use a zip if you can avoid it; if you do, use a good quality strong one. Any trouser pattern for a formal pair of trousers will demonstrate a more traditional way of making a fly opening.

Flap-front opening

Sew the centre-front seam from crotch to waist. Cut two slits either side of the centre front. Face the whole centre section and add a lap to the outside slits. Button the front flap over the lapped slits.

Pockets

The quickest side pockets are made by cutting them all in one with the side seam and sewing them together at the same time as the side seam. Press

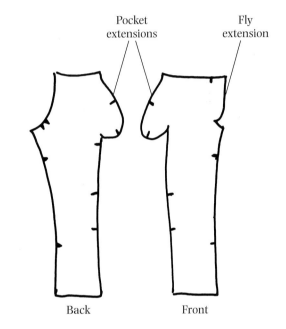

Back   Front

The trousers.

Flap-front trousers.

the seam and pockets from the right side with the pockets facing forward. When they look right, and are lying smoothly within the side seam, pin the lower edge through all thicknesses and secure with a 2-cm (about five-eighths of an inch) bar of stitching, to keep them in place. This will also strengthen them when the hands are in the pockets. Once again, the formal trouser pattern will show you the traditional way of making pockets.

Trouser Back Seams
Double-stitch the first 20cm (8in) from crotch to waist and stitch the rest less firmly until after the fitting. This centre-back seam is the easiest place to adjust the fit of trousers.

Crotches
Make certain that the cross formed by the inside leg seam and the back and front seam is very securely stitched, as this is the place where trousers are most likely to split. Double-stitch all seams and make sure that there is an adequate seam allowance, and that there is no danger of the cloth fraying.

USEFUL TIPS

Matching In all situations where pockets, decorative features, and so on, need to be symmetrical, position and stitch them before the garment is made up. It is much easier to be exact when the work can be laid flat.

Braiding It is often difficult to be accurate if you pin braid in position before you sew it. Draw its position with chalk or pencil and use that as a guide. Braid before the garment is made up if it is easier, for instance, round the cuff of a narrow sleeve or round a pocket or flap.

Gathering Gather with the largest machine stitch. Sew two parallel rows 1cm (half an inch) apart and attach the gathers between the rows. It may sounds as though this method would take longer than a single row but, in fact, it makes it quicker as it is easier to be accurate.

Buttonholes It takes a bit of practice to sew machine buttonholes but it is a skill well worth mastering. Keep the distance between each button symmetrical. It is easier to sew neat, strong buttonholes on stiff cloth so, if the fabric is floppy, sandwich a strip of iron-on stiffening between the two layers of cloth. Do not cut the buttonholes too big, as they tend to get bigger with use. Men's clothes traditionally button left over right and women's clothes right over left.

Buttons Use strong button thread and sew buttons on firmly. Make the buttonholes first, line up the front in the buttoned position, and mark where to sew the buttons with a pencil or chalk mark. When sewing by hand, be extra careful to fasten on and fasten off your thread securely.

Fastenings by machine Buttons, larger press studs and big hooks and eyes can be sewn by machine if it has the facility to disengage the feed dog and does a zigzag stitch. The machine instruction leaflet will tell you if this is possible. You will break and blunt a few needles while learning, but will ultimately save yourself hours of boring, finger-wearing labour if you get it right. Most modern machines will do this, and, once you have struggled through the first three or four, it becomes quick and easy. It also saves your fingers when sewing on heavy cloth or leather. The machine method is more useful for larger fastenings on heavy cloth; it is not delicate enough for chiffon or other lightweight cloths.

Lace Fine lace or ruffles will often gather automatically if you straight-stitch the top edge with the machine tension loose, or using a long stitch.

Pockets It takes less time to create pockets when you are making the garment than to add them at the dress rehearsal when you suddenly realize that someone needs to produce a snuff box from his waistcoat. Put them in from the beginning if you think there is any chance they might be needed, particularly when working on a show such as a pantomime or a farce, where there tend to be lots of props. It is quite rare for dancers to use pockets. Have an arrangement with the stage manager to note the size of the props that are to go in the pockets and to give you a list after each day's rehearsal.

Temporary seams When you are doubtful whether a seam will be permanent, and suspect it might be changed at the fitting, sew on the longest machine stitch. Leave several centimetres (a couple of inches) of thread at each end of the seam and do not fasten it off. You will be able to unpick it easily, or sew over your temporary stitching with a smaller, firmer stitch when you are sure all is well.

Pinning Pins stay in more firmly if passed three or four times through the cloth. Use safety pins at fittings if you are worried that the pins will fall out between fitting and workroom. A magnet is a great help. It enables you to collect pins easily when you knock them on to the floor, and you can chuck the pins at it to collect when you are working in frenzied rhythm and cannot bear to stop your whirring machine even for a moment.

Threads Trim threads as you go, otherwise you may find you do not know which ends belong to gathering threads and temporary seams.

Hanging help Put two loops in the waistband of skirts and breeches, or trousers without creases, so that they can be hung on skirt hangers. Put tape loops on accessories if dressing rooms are crowded, so that they can be kept on the hanger with the costume. Sew tape loops in the waist of a wide-necked bodice that would slip off a hanger, and hang it upside-down. Sew loops in the backs of jackets and coats, or anything that is likely to be hung on a coat hook rather than a hanger. Do anything you can to make it easy for costumes to be hung up and stay up, so that they are less likely to be trampled underfoot. Younger actors who are not used to wearing trousers with front and back creases may need to be taught how to hang them so that they retain the creases.

Scraps and offcuts Keep a bag of offcuts for patching and mending and give them to whoever is looking after the costumes once the show is running. Pass on any warnings about cloth that you have found difficult to press, and information about which colours might run in the wash to the person in charge of the maintenance of the costumes.

DANGER POINTS

Seam splitting This is most likely at the crotch, back seam on tight trousers, underarm seam, elbows on tight sleeves, thigh seam on tight breeches, the back of armholes, and any places where three or more seams meet.

Fastening off Always sew a few stitches forward and back on any permanent line of stitching so that it cannot unravel itself. Fasten off hand-sewing with three or four small stitches on top of each other.

Tight armholes Armholes that are tight are extremely uncomfortable to wear and can cause painful rashes and sore places. Acting is a sweaty business and extra room and careful fitting means less sweat and less washing. Ask the actor at the fitting to fold their arms and stretch and wriggle to make sure there is enough room for movement.

Long skirts The hem of the skirt should just clear the toes, unless the skirt is held right away from the body by a crinoline. It can dip slightly at the sides, as long as the front does not catch under the toe when the actress is walking forward; check this at a fitting. Put a loop on a train so that it can be hooked over the wrist. This will save the train being trodden on and is useful backstage even if it is not needed onstage.

Wrinkled tights and sagging trousers Braces do not have to be thick or adjustable as long as they are strong enough for the garment they are supporting. They are an excellent way of keeping trousers, tights, breeches and even skirts up, particularly on plump or big-bellied actors. They stay on the shoulders best if crossed at the back.

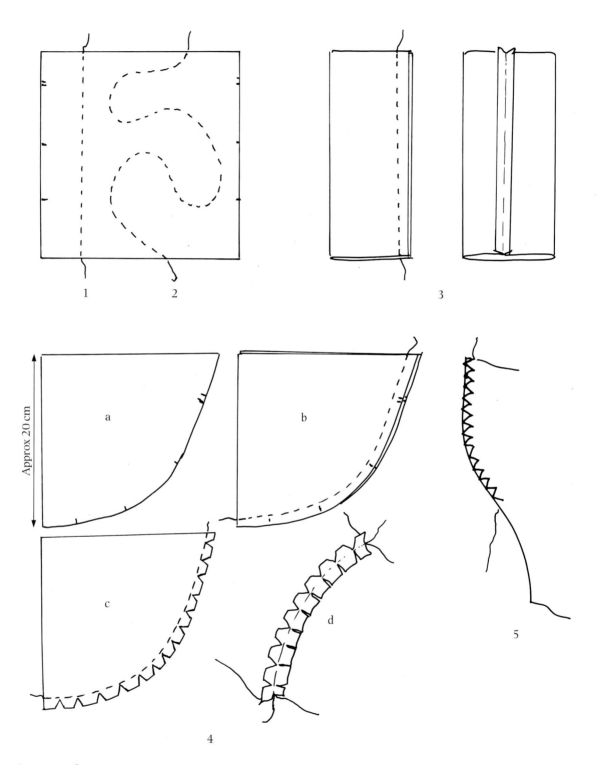

Diagrams for test section.

Padding All the wadding used to make paddings must be washable and tumble-dryable. Padding gets soaked through with sweat and must be easy to wash and dry. Make padding as light as possible and cut it well back from armholes, neck and groin. It may need to be made on a leotard-shaped base to stop it riding up. Stab through all layers with strong thread and a long needle, to prevent the stuffing moving inside the covers. A very small thickness of padding can make a big difference to the shape of the body, so build up the layers gradually until you have created the shape you want. Always make the padding first so that the actor can wear it at every fitting for the costume that goes over it.

TEST

Use the diagrams opposite to cut out a piece of flat cloth big enough to work on, about 40cm (16in) square.

1. Sew a straight line. If you cannot sew a straight line, practise using the markings on the footplate of the machine as a guide. Rule a line on a piece of fabric and follow it.
2. Follow a curve. Draw a scroll shape on a piece of cloth and follow it.
3. Make a straight seam. Sew the seam 2cm (five-eighths of an inch) from the edge, matching the notches as you go. Press the seam open
4. Sew a curved seam.
   a) Cut shapes.
   b) Sew the seam 1cm (quarter of an inch) from the edge, matching notches.
   c) Cut little triangles in the seam allowance to allow it to spread out or contract when pressed flat, so that it does not wrinkle.
   d) Press the seam smooth. You may have to press it over a wodge of cloth to allow for the curves in the cloth. If it will not lie flat when pressed, you have not cut enough slits and triangles.
5. Practise zigzagging to finish off the edges. The left-hand swing of the needle should pierce the cloth and the right-hand swing should just clear the edge of the cloth, so that the thread binds round the raw edge of the fabric.

With these few techniques and the various methods of fastening at your fingertips, you can at least get started; you can pick up the rest as you go along. A basic book of simple sewing techniques is helpful if you do not have a great deal of experience. Every single thing you make will teach you something new and you will carry on learning until the end of your sewing life. You will develop quick ways to put on collars and cuffs, and your own favourite way of boning a corset. You will recognize the time in the costume construction when you can think about something else, and be aware of those times that call for total concentration. You will go on making mistakes but, with luck, you will not make the same one twice.

Learn to trust your eyes and your instinct. Remember that you are working at arm's length from the garment but the audience will see your creations from much further away. If you cannot see that a hem has been stitched by machine and not by hand, the audience will not see it either. If you feel something looks very wrong in the workroom, it will probably look wrong on stage. When you see a costume you have made onstage you will be conscious of every fault; you need to learn to look with the eyes of the audience and decide whether they will notice, and whether you should put it right. There are some faults that are glaring onstage, but are hard to see in a crowded workroom. They are most likely to be in a position of contrasts: the wobbly hem of a dress seen against the light background, an unevenly spaced line of dark buttons on a light dress, the two shoulder-gathers of leg-of-mutton sleeves giving an uneven silhouette to the shoulder line. Sleeves or trousers that are too short or too long are more obvious than a waist that is a little loose or a collar that is a bit tight.

The actors never see themselves onstage, so it is not unreasonable for them to worry about costume details that you may know the audience will never see. Actors sit in the dressing room, surrounded by mirrors, while they wait to go onstage and look at themselves in close-up, and with the same critical eye that we all have for our own appearance. A loose waist may make the actress feel frumpy and unattractive, but no one in the audience will notice it; be as sympathetic and helpful as you have time to be. Actors work best in costumes that are strong, well made and comfortable, and, most important of all, make them feel right for their role.

FITTINGS

Fittings for costumes represent an important step in the rehearsal period of a play. They are useful to designers, because they offer the opportunity to see the costume on the actor, and to change details that do not work. They give the maker vital information about the fit and progress of the costume, and they give the actors a chance to see themselves as the audience will see them.

The Designer

The designer has a picture of the costume in her mind – the same picture she has drawn on paper. The one she sees at the fitting may differ in many respects. The actor may be the perfect physical type

Early stages in the life of a costume.

*An eyepatch is made
practical for stage
use by the addition of
a gauze panel.*

for the role and be delighted with the way he looks. The costume may look better than the designer imagined and the cloth, colour and cut may surpass the picture created in her mind. In this case, there is no problem.

On the other hand, the whole thing may be a miserable disappointment. The actor may be a different shape from the imagined character and feel the costume makes him look wrong for the role; the fabric may not be quite the same as the samples and the actual construction of the costume may be uncomfortable and badly made. When this happens, the designer must make snap decisions. It is destructive to make criticisms if the problem cannot be rectified but it is vital to suggest improvements if there is any chance that they can be put into practice. The designer must assess the time available, and the experience and skill of the maker, and find out whether there is money in the budget to make alterations. It helps if the designer has experience of cutting and making and can make practical suggestions for changes. She must do all this without destroying the confidence of the actor in the costume, and either enraging the maker or reducing her to tears. In truly disastrous cases, when the costume is an irreparable disaster, the production manager may have to be asked to

step in and assess the situation. Designers often work with makers they know and trust whenever they can, to be sure of avoiding these sorts of situations.

The Maker

The maker uses fittings to check that the costume fits well in all respects and to ensure that the actor can move with ease in the clothes. Hemlines and sleeve lengths can be set, and adjustments to make the costume fit perfectly will be pinned in. The maker must be allowed enough time to make all the adjustments before the designer starts suggesting alterations. Fittings can be difficult for the maker if there is discussion and gesture and movement going on between the actor and the designer, and she is left to set a collar in place or pin a hem on a constantly moving body.

It is a wonderful feeling for a maker when she has re-created on a moving body a costume that first appeared as a picture on a flat piece of paper. It is even more satisfying when the designer believes that she has got the look that she originally imagined, and the actor is delighted. It can be deeply distressing when things go wrong, and difficult not to get angry or be upset by an adverse reaction to your work, particularly when you have

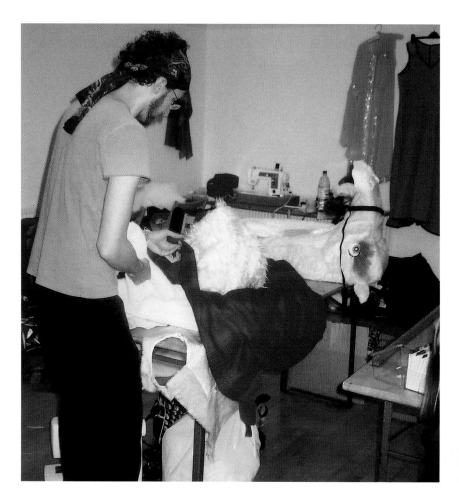

An animal-skin maker at work on Camilla the Camel.

struggled through half the night to get it ready on time. Most things can be put right somehow; again, the production manager can be asked to help sort out a relationship between designer and maker that has gone awry.

The Costume Supervisor

In larger companies, where there may be many different people employed in making the costumes, hats, wigs, and so on, for a production, a costume supervisor is employed to liaise between the designer and makers. She will be at the fittings, at times standing in for the designer, and will arrange for the makers working on different parts of the costume to be there at the same time when appropriate.

The Actor

An experienced actor uses the fitting as a building block in the work he is doing as he builds the character he will present to the audience. It is impossible to over-emphasize how much the physical appearance of the characters affects the audience's understanding of the play. Actors know this, and this knowledge is strengthened by the feelings they have themselves towards the costumed figure they see in the mirror. In common with the designer and the maker, they need the time at fittings to take in the look of the costume, to analyse the way it makes them feel, and to move about and get an idea of the weight and swing of the cloth.

The picture the actor has built up in his mind

during rehearsals may be very different from the one he sees at the fitting. He may not have seen the design since the read-through; in some cases, he may not have seen it at all. Actors usually know if a costume feels right or not and there can be some pretty stormy and emotional scenes when actors and designers disagree. It very often happens that calm discussion, a cup of tea and some quite minor changes can make all parties a great deal happier. Good communication between actors, designers and makers, particularly when the designs are first shown and discussed, make fittings constructive and exciting occasions.

The Freelance Maker

Freelance makers are contracted by a company to make the costumes in their own workroom. They are often specialists – for example, milliners, animal-skin makers, boot, armour or mask makers – who work for many different production companies. The arrangements and money matters will be sorted out by the production manager; in some cases the materials will be bought by the designer or costume supervisor. In other situations, particularly those, such as mask making, that involve specialist supplies, the materials will be bought by the maker and the money reclaimed from the company. A web of these costume specialists exists wherever there is theatre and film making. Some of them advertise, but most get work through personal recommendation, or have been affiliated with a particular company or costume supervisor or designer for years.

Arranging Fittings

Times for fittings are arranged between the maker or costume supervisor and the stage manager, although in smaller companies there may be less formal ways of going about it. It can be difficult for directors to spare actors from a busy rehearsal schedule and it is best if fittings can be arranged during the time that actors are not wanted in the rehearsal room. In many companies, the actors must be paid for fittings that take place outside the normal working day, so there can be a juggling act within the schedule to make sure that no working hours and no money are used up unnecessarily.

In a less formally run company, it can work quite well if the wardrobe department puts up a notice on the company notice board of everyone who needs to be seen, together with an approximate timescale for each fitting, and asks the actors to come to Wardrobe when they are not onstage. Try to keep to the time you have suggested for each fitting, so that rehearsal time will not be wasted by the company having to wait around onstage for actors who are still half-dressed in the Wardrobe. If your notice-board requests fail, you can enlist the help of the stage manager to schedule a fitting space into the actor's working day.

Doing It All

Smaller companies may combine the jobs of designer, maker and costume supervisor under the blanket title of 'Wardrobe'. Wardrobe may be one hard-working person, or several people who work at home making and fitting the costumes away from the theatre. Amateur companies may spread their rehearsal and preparation time over several months, and it will be left up to the maker to arrange fittings with the actors. The production manager, or whoever manages the budget, will provide information about the financial arrangements for fittings that take place outside the theatre. There will be phone calls to make arrangements, travel expenses for actors and makers, a mileage rate and parking if there is car travel, and actors may need to be paid if they are called for fittings outside their contracted hours. It is a legal requirement that children are chaperoned at fittings if they are under sixteen.

8 OTHER WARDROBE SKILLS

There is a more to creating costumes than cutting and sewing. The job has little to do with everyday dressmaking, although a costume maker does need to be able to cut and sew. He or she must also be able to glue and saw, paint and dye, budget, shop and keep accounts, and organize hiring and fittings. The workload has to be organized to keep every member of a large concern working fast at the skills at which they are best. For this to happen, the shopping, the cutting and the fittings have to be re-juggled on a day-to-day basis, according to the progress of the work and the ever-shifting vagaries of directors, actors and rehearsal. The likelihood of never knowing exactly how the work will progress next day is sometimes infuriating, but the job is never boring.

HAIR

The effect of the best costume can be ruined if it is topped by the wrong hairstyle. Costume designers design the shape of the hair when they decide on the costume, but that ideal style can be difficult to achieve when there is a limited budget. It is very helpful if the actor has the length of hair that can be styled in the manner of the period. Long hair, particularly for women, allows more possibilities, and extra hairpieces can be used if the actor does not have enough natural hair.

Good wigs are expensive and need to be dressed regularly and expertly if they are to look realistic.

OPPOSITE: *Alan Howard as Oedipus, Tanya Moodie as Antigone and Clare Swinburne as Ismene in* **The Oedipus Plays.** *Photo: Robbie Jack*

RIGHT: *Adjusting the hair on an animal mask.*

Some men and women will be willing to dye and cut their hair for a role – in this case they should have a clear picture of the style to show to the hairdresser. Most actors prefer to use their own hair. Keep this possibility open by asking actors not to cut their hair until they have seen the design for their costume, and discussed the hairstyle for their role.

Men may prefer to grow their own sideburns, beards and moustaches rather than fiddle around with spirit gum and toupee tape before every performance. It can take some men longer than others to grow facial hair, so if the rehearsal period is short, contact them as soon as is practical to discuss the matter.

MAKE-UP

Actors never see their own make-up onstage. They peer in the dressing-room mirror and see their

*An actor makes up
for the show.*

reflection at arm's length. The face they see reflected there may look very different from the face the audience sees from the back row of the gallery in the glare of the stage lights. Eyeliner that enhances the eyes in the mirror may appear to close them to slits under certain lighting and a jaw line that seems natural in the dressing room may look flat and undefined under the strong light. Eyebrows may vanish, giving a skull-like look to the face. The costume designer and wardrobe department can advise when the right effect is achieved.

Make-up varies with period, and a 'natural' make-up for a young girl in the eighteenth century will not be the same as a 'natural' make-up for a 1920s flapper. Drawings or photographs of a suitable make-up will help the actor create a good effect. The made-up face will become part of the costume design in cases where the designer imagines a stylized or particular face. Companies with money for extra crew, or amateur companies, may employ a make-up artist to work with the actors on their make-up for a production. It is usual for actors to supply their own make-up unless something out of the ordinary has been designed for their character.

MILLINERY

Hats crop up in most projects, in some way or other, and fall roughly into four categories: soft, hard, felt and straw. It is a great help to have a head shape to work on when you are making or altering hats. A 5-litre paint tin wrapped in thick cloth will work as some sort of substitute for a head block, and is more convenient than pinning your own head in front of the mirror.

Soft Hats (Cloth Bonnets, Berets, Pull-On Caps and Turbans)
The shaping of cloth caps and bonnets is created by the cut of the cloth and its seams and gathers. For those who find it difficult to make up their own pattern, there are commercial patterns for modern hats and dressing up, which give basic shapes that can be adapted for period use. The easiest way to cut a pattern is to make a rough example in waste cloth.

Hard Hats (Helmets, Bowlers, Top Hats and Uniform Peaked Caps)
Formal hats, such as the bowler and the top hat, are the most difficult to make from scratch. The

OTHER WARDROBE SKILLS

most successful way to achieve a convincing look is to buy the nearest shape you can find to the one you want, and alter, paint or decorate it. It is possible to stretch most hats to a larger size by removing the inside band, steaming the hat over a kettle and stretching it gently; you cannot stretch much or the crispness of the shape will be lost. Helmets, whether on a Trojan warrior or the Home Guard, must look hard and heavy. It is easier to bodge up a helmet from the dim and distant past as few people are sure what they looked like. The tin hat of the Second World War or the police helmet

Gathers or elastic

Mob cap

Gathers or elastic

Turn back

Full cap

Hood

Point A can be elongated to touch the floor, to tuck into a belt or to wind around the neck.

Hood worn as a hat with cowl folded on top.

Variations on the bag hat

Soft hats. The basic patterns for all these can be adapted to many different styles.

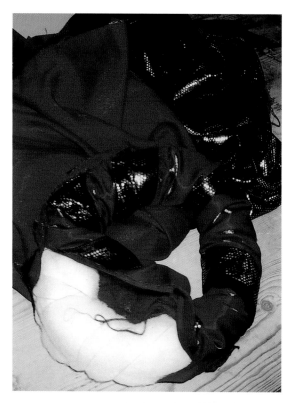

Making and adapting hats
ABOVE: *A straw-hat brim is stitched by machine before re-cutting.*
LEFT: *The rolled brim of a hat is stuffed with wadding.*
BELOW: *A new hat is made using an old fez as a base.*

of the riot squad must look more realistic, and an army surplus shop may prove a better starting point than the charity shop.

Felt Hats

If you hold a felt hat (a trilby or cloth hat that holds its own shape) over a panful of steaming water, it goes floppy and soft, regaining its former stiffness as it cools. This means that felt hats can be stretched, curled, dented, and reshaped in all sorts of ways. The felt does not fray so the brims can be cut to a new shape, or a larger brim cut to extend a brim that is too small. The crown measurement can be made smaller by making a hat band of the correct size, slipping it over the crown, and steaming the hat to shrink it inside the band; you may have to encourage the shrinkage by ironing over a wodge of cloth or a tailor's ham.

Straw Hats (Boaters, Sunhats and Panamas)

Most of the shapes you are likely to need are still being made today and will just need the appropriate decoration in the way of hat bands, feathers and flowers, to suit your purpose. If you have to cut a straw hat, draw the new shape and zigzag inside the line before you cut so that the weave does not unravel.

CORSETS

Making a corset in the traditional way is complicated, time-consuming and difficult. It can be learnt by working from an original pattern in one of the many books about the subject. A good corset affects not only the appearance of the costume, as all the stresses that would otherwise be apparent in the fabric of the dress are absorbed by the corset, but also the way the actor moves. There may not be the skill and time available to make these complicated garments, but a simpler method can produce adequate results and is certainly better than nothing at all. There are patterns available in the fancy-dress section of pattern books or you can begin by using the pattern for any bodice that is cut with a seam over the bust as well as at the sides.

Cut the bodice pieces in strong cotton fabric, adding an extra seam at centre-front and centre-back if the pattern does not have one. Add extra length and width if necessary, to carry the corset over the hips. Pin the seams together, fit it on the actor, and adjust it so that it fits as closely as a second skin. Use the fitted bodice as a pattern, but stitch all vertical seams slightly inside your pins so that the bodice is a little too small and will shape the body of the actor when fastened.

The following hints will help you in your corset making and fitting:

- Use hook-and-eye tape to fasten; it is strong, and you can stitch it on by machine and bone through the channel it produces.
- If you need to lace the corset, the eyelets available in haberdashery shops will last better if you interface the fabric with iron-on interfacing, or glue the layers of fabric together before you punch the holes.
- If you cannot find corset laces (available from very well-stocked haberdashery shops), use flat, narrow shoe laces. You may have to stitch them together to get enough length.
- Make the channels for the corset bones as close-fitting as possible, to prevent the bones twisting and shifting.
- Cover the ends of bones, pad them with tape, and set them a little below the armpit on the side seam. Be particularly careful to cover the ends of the boning that is sold by the metre; little jabbing sharps of plastic work their way through the casing and stab like pins.
- A well-fitting corset always feels too tight for the first two minutes until the body settles into place.
- Most actresses like wearing a corset when the role demands it and are prepared to put up with the slight discomfort of such a close-fitting garment.
- Most singers are worried by corsets and will prefer to sacrifice the look of the costume in order to keep the full expansion of their ribs and diaphragm.
- A dancer's corset must allow her arms freedom of movement as well as her body and be as

unrestricting as possible. It helps if it can stop above the waist, not have shoulder straps and have light and flexible boning.

BRUSHWORK

A costume can have as much glue and paintbrush work as needlework. It can be quicker to stencil pattern on to a costume than to appliqué a design with fabric, and it is certainly speedier to glue on sequins than to sew them by hand. As a general rule, paint will need to dry without stiffening the fabric. There are many fabric paints and dyes, found in art and craft shops, that stay supple and are colourfast for washing. Some of them need to be set by steam or heat, so it is important to read the instructions for use and to make sure the colours you buy will be good for the job. Ordinary emulsion paint or car spray-paint will last well on fabric, but it will stiffen cloth unless it is applied very thinly. There are times, particularly when making hats or puppets, when you want to stiffen the cloth without changing its colour. This can be achieved by painting or soaking with PVA adhesive and letting the cloth dry while it is arranged in the desired shape. You can buy a spray made for stiffening window blinds, which will have the same effect. Specialist shops that sell theatrical supplies offer a wide assortment of colours and dyes, glitter and UV paints, and particular glues for different purposes. If you do not have one in your area, it is worth having a look at their mail-order catalogues.

DYEING

It may not be possible to find the colour you want in the fabric you need. Dye for home use, which is excellent for theatre purposes and comes in a wide variety of colours, is easy to use and has clear instructions on the packets. The most difficult thing about dyeing is guessing whether the cloth will take the dye. Natural fibres absorb colour well. Man-made fibres tend to be more difficult and it may be impossible to achieve anything other than a pastel shade without specialist equipment. Many natural-fibre garments are sewn with polyester thread, which may reject the dye, so that you end up with bright white stitching on a dark-coloured garment; check that this will not matter before you start. Use pure cotton thread to stitch costumes if you plan to dye them later. Some fabrics, such as Lycra, will accept dye better when boiled, so they

The dye pot — the light colour absorbs the dye, the black stays black.

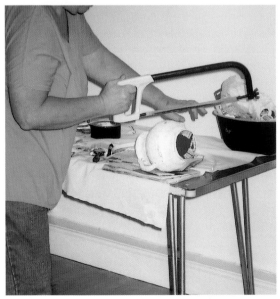

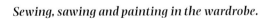

Sewing, sawing and painting in the wardrobe.

Ageing costumes with dye and paint.

test fabric before you can see the true colour of the finished result.

BREAKING DOWN

Costumes may need to look old and worn, even though they have been newly made. Imagine a jacket that has been worn throughout twenty years' worth of hard work. The edges of the collar, the cuffs and the area near the buttons may be worn, greasy and frayed; the fastenings will have been buttoned and unbuttoned countless times and the buttonholes will have become stretched out of shape. Some of the buttons may have been replaced by new ones, which do not quite match or are hanging by a longer thread. The elbows may have worn through and be patched or darned. Years of hands or objects in the pockets will have made the front hang unevenly. The cloth will have the rubbed and irregular look of a garment that has been wet and dry and wet and dry over and over again. The parts of the garment that have seen the most sun, such as the outside of the coat sleeves and the shoulders, will have faded more than the cloth of the inside arm, which has spent most of its life in shadow. Sweat and body grease leave marks on armpits and collars. Breaking down a new jacket to look as it has had a similar wealth of experience is a particular Wardrobe skill.

All sorts of means are used to simulate the years of wear: wetting and drying with weights in the pockets; crumpling and pulling; painting stains and dipping the cloth unevenly in a dye close to the original colour; bleaching areas with a weak solution of bleach or colour stripper. Candle wax, shoe polish or oil can be rubbed on collars and cuffs, and a stiff scrubbing brush, a little wire brush like those sold for cleaning suede shoes, or even sandpaper can roughen edges and patches. Threads can be pulled out to make frayed holes or hems.

MAKING THINGS LIGHT

Costumes, hats and accessories can become heavy. Clothes in the past were much heavier than they are today and most accurate reproductions of

cannot be dyed to a deep shade in an automatic washing machine but must be coloured in a dyepot or boiler.

To guess if a cloth will take dye, mix a jam jar of dye of a strong colour and dip a sample of the cloth into the pot. If the cloth sucks up the colour readily and does not rinse clean easily, you will have no trouble. If the cloth turns a paler shade than you would hope, you may have to boil the sample to see if that improves matters. If the sample takes little colour, or rinses clean in cold water afterwards, you may not be able to dye it without expert help.

Dark colours can never be dyed to a lighter shade, although there are commercial products that strip fabric of colour to prepare it for dyeing. Bleach will take the colour out of fabric but may rot the fibres. Dyes can be mixed to obtain the exact shade you want, but you must rinse and dry the upper-class dress of the last six or seven hundred years would be too cumbersome for an actor to work in; a woman in a crinoline might have had forty or fifty metres of cloth, braid, whalebone and steel laced and tied on to her body. No stage actor today would be happy to work with such constriction and weight hampering her movement and breathing. The weight of a costume, and the sort of movement that will be used in a production, has to be considered by the maker.

There are many tricks to make costumes appear heavier and thicker than they are. Fabrics that trap air (think of bubble-wrap) make light cloth appear heavy, as do fibres that are in themselves bulky but not heavy (think of cotton wool or a duvet). Three of the most powerful suggestions of the thickness of an object are the way it hangs on the body, the apparent solidity of the folds, and a slight roundness at the hems and edges. Cloth weight can be suggested by interlining and there are many interlining, light wadded and man-made fabrics and stiffenings that can be used instead of the supple shiny lining used on everyday clothes. Edges of the cloth can be made to look thicker by inserting a thin strip of wadding or soft cord within the hem, by outlining the edge with a cord or braid, or binding the edge with a binding a little heavier than the main cloth.

Net is cheap and light, comes in many colours and, when stiff-gathered, creates an underskirt that can build up a petticoat without adding to its weight. Elaborate hats can become too heavy to be practical unless care is taken to keep the fabrics light, even when they appear to use up a lot of air space. Feathers are an excellent example; a peacock's feather can be a metre long, yet the quill that nature has invented to support it weighs next to nothing and the airy fronds that make its shape and pattern create a dazzling effect with scarcely any substance.

PUPPETRY AND ANIMATED OBJECTS

With the growth of object theatre, where no precise line can be drawn between props and costumes, animated objects have become a part of many productions. When a specialist is not employed to design and make the puppets, they are likely to be constructed either in the props workshop or in the costume department. Alternatively, they may be the result of a joint project between the two. Marionettes and glove puppets are only a small part of the story. Puppets can be chairs or dustbins or bread rolls or lampshades, or indeed any object that is animated onstage. An experienced puppet maker may be able to make a puppet, give it to an equally experienced animator and achieve an acceptable result. When actors who are not trained puppeteers are animating puppets and objects onstage, the designer, animator and makers must all work together to achieve the best outcome. Experiments can be carried out in rehearsal and in the workroom with sticks and paper, clothes and cloth, plastic and wood. The shape, weight and size and the means of manipulation will then have been decided, and there will be a practical starting point for the design and creation of the object as the audience will see it.

MASKS

Masks represent another specialist area that falls, when a mask maker is not employed, into the workrooms of the Wardrobe or the prop maker. The more decorative masks, such as those designed as part of the costume for a masked ball, will usually be made in the Wardrobe. Good effects can be achieved by extending and decorating the basic domino shape that is sold in party shops today. Masks that are used to give expression and character to the performance call for more sculptural skills.

Actors working in masked drama need to rehearse in their mask as it exerts a powerful influence on the development of the character and the movement of the actor's body. It can be difficult to talk or sing in a mask – any alterations necessary to facilitate the production of the voice will become apparent through rehearsal. It will usually become the responsibility of the wardrobe department to sort out any minor problems that occur. Masks must stay snugly in place, but not

Working with papier mâché, cloth and net to create 'dancing stone' costumes ... and the costumes dancing!

clash with an actor's eyelashes when she blinks, or press on the bridge of the nose or on the cheekbones. These problems can usually be resolved by glueing thin patches of sponge or padding in a position where it will alter the angle of the mask and stop it pressing on the face.

An actor's field of vision is narrowed by most masks, which make it impossible to look down without bending the head, or to look to the side without turning. The field of vision is widest when the eyeholes are large and the mask lies close to the upper face. It sometimes works well to enlarge the eyeholes and make up the actor's eyes to match the mask. The places where the mask gives way to the real skin are the danger areas. The closer the mask lies against the skin the better, as any gap creates a dark line of shadow, which will need to be hidden by hair or disguised with make-up.

*Painting puppet
heads.*

DEPORTMENT AND ETIQUETTE

The research that costume designers and makers
do into period costume, and their interest in the
subject, means that they soak up information
about the etiquette and movement associated with
the fashions of each era and the way accessories
are used. The handshake of the 1940s woman in
her emancipated, square-shouldered dress would
seem ridiculous and inappropriate to the
eighteenth-century lady in her elbow-length
ruffled sleeves; the stride of the nineteenth-
century dandy in his tight pantaloons and light
pumps is a world away from the lope of a young
man in the low-crutched, hip-slung baggy trousers
and trainers of the early twenty-first century.
When there is no other movement expert in the
building, the Wardrobe can often be relied on to
teach actors how to use a fan, how to curtsey in a
crinoline or how to offer a snuff box.

MAINTENANCE

Acting is a dirty, sweaty, energetic business and
costumes become worn, torn and smelly unless
they are taken care of. This is a daily task for the
people responsible for looking after the costumes
during the running if the show. Costumes may

have to be re-made in a long run or if a role is re-
cast, but most of the work, apart from cleaning,
will involve repairs to split seams, lost fastenings
and the occasional patch or darn.

It is useful to have a supply of spare tights,
handkerchiefs, hairbands, grips and pins, gloves
and socks, and any other small items that may get
lost easily or are likely to need to be replaced. It is
also helpful if actors wear cotton T-shirts under
their costumes to absorb the worst of the sweat;
the neck can be cut down so that it does not show
under an open-neck costume and the T-shirt can
be replaced when washing costumes is impossible
between shows, for example, on matinee days.

When working with a large company, it can be
quite a tricky and hurried business to collect, sort,
wash, dry and return costumes to the right
dressing rooms, particularly when there is a show
in the evening and a matinee next day. The
following ideas will help:

- Leave a bag or basket in the dressing room so
  that actors have a place to put their dirty
  washing and you do not have to spend time
  rooting around looking for it.
- Divide colours into light and dark and try to
  keep white and cream cloth separate from other
  colours.

- You can speed up a slow washing machine by pouring the water in from a jug or bucket, instead of letting it trickle in slowly. You can hear the sound change as the trickle stops when you have poured in enough.
- Read the washing machine instructions and find out the quickest cycle.
- The coolest wash is usually the quickest and the least wearing to the clothes, but may have a less powerful spinning action.
- It can be quicker to hand-wash a garment and rinse and spin it in the washing machine.
- A net bag with a drawstring top makes the job of washing and sorting socks easier.
- Some soap powders contain a chemical which shows up in ultraviolet light.
- Tumble driers dry clothes more quickly if you put a dry bath towel in with the wet clothes. It also speeds things up if you take the clothes out and shake them half-way through.
- The quicker you get the clothes out of washer or drier when the cycle has finished, the easier they are to iron.
- If you iron the parts of the clothes the audience does not see, you are doing it for the actor and not the audience.

- Arrange early collection of costumes that have to be dry-cleaned outside the theatre building so that you have time to rectify any problems if the cleaners let you down.
- It is a risky practice to allow actors to take costumes out of the building.
- Have a place on the company notice board where actors can leave messages about costumes that need mending.
- Take comfort in the fact that costumes always look cleaner under stage light than they do in the dressing room.

SEEING POSSIBILITIES

It is not always possible to re-create the picture in the design as a finished garment. Designs edge as near as they can to a vision in the imagination of their creator, but they are two-dimensional and do not move. The skill of the maker transforms the ideas into something that will be practical to wear and can be realized with the resources that are available to the project. The costume maker who is short of time and money becomes adept at finding ways of saving both.

There is no reason to make a whole shirt when

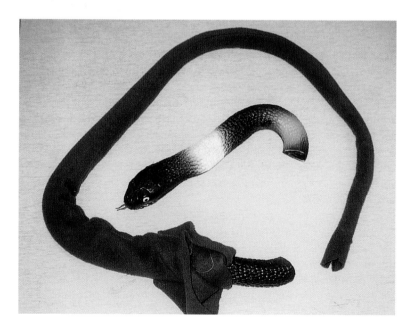

Making a rat's tail from a rubber snake covered with cloth ...

only the collar and cuffs will show and they can be attached to any old shirt. There is no particular reason to use calico to cut patterns and linings. Although it is traditional, and costume makers have used it for years, it is more expensive than second-hand cotton sheets, which have the added benefit of being pre-shrunk. A wander round a car-boot sale will offer endless accessible, affordable solutions to problems. A broken carbon-fibre fishing rod can become the light strong spines that support the wings of a giant bird; a boa can be plucked for its feathers; a dozen baseball hats with an obsolete logo may become the base, with the peaks removed, for the headdresses of the Greek chorus. You need leather gaiters – chop up a pair of women's boots; you must have masses of bangles and beads for the Sultan's harem – destroy a beaded door-curtain to make them. If the fabric of a car seat can look like metal, there is no reason at all for the audience to know it is not metal when they see it as a breastplate on a Roman General. You have to tell your eyes to see things for what they look like and not for what they are, when you are searching for imaginative solutions.

... and painting frog feet on scuba-diving boots.

ORGANIZATION

The date, and often the exact time, when costumes must be completed is set by the stern schedules of the technical and dress rehearsals and the first night. A single actor in a production may be allocated twenty or thirty, or even more, separate items, ranging from the T-shirt he sweats into underneath his costume to his false beard, from his ring and cufflinks to his overcoat. Most of these he will wear onstage for the first time at the tech. In the ideal world – so rarely inhabited by a theatre company – these should be ready for this first costumed rehearsal, although the last possible moment all these items must be waiting in the dressing room is the first night.

All the work needed to provide a costume can be completed in time only if there is a system in the Wardrobe for checking and storing the finished items, and listing the work still to be done. All items must be budgeted for, found or made, and fitted. The petty-cash float, the receipts that account for it, order forms or requisition notes and invoices must have their place. An office corner, even if it is little more than a pin-board and a cardboard box, must be arranged. It is essential to have somewhere for the Wardrobe staff to dump anything to do with financial matters; they can be sorted when the hustle and urgency of the last stages of rehearsal have passed.

9 ACCESSORIES

The clothes are only part of the costume. It takes more than a few items of clothing to create the picture that will give the audience an insight into the life of the play. In some productions, it may be impossible or undesirable for the actors to wear naturalistic costume. In such cases, accessories and props may be used to give an impression of the period and the characters. Accessories can be changed quickly and easily. Many productions ask the actors to play multiple roles, and to move from role to role without leaving the stage. An actor changing his trousers on stage can look clumsy or comic, and it is difficult to retain internal concentration while fumbling with buttons and zips. The same actor can buckle on a sword belt in full sight of the audience without looking or feeling at all ridiculous, and the audience will find it easier to believe in him as another character because they have seen the change taking place.

Accessories belong to particular periods and the gestures that are so often associated with them are grist to the actor's mill. Think of the alluring movements of the hand and arm that the fan encourages, and that particular posture and gesture of the mobile-phone user as he stands on a street corner. A woman gathers up the skirt of her apron and wipes her hands when the doorbell rings, and the young man stands, elbow out, shoulders squared, with his hand on the hilt of his sword. The costume designer gives the actors and the audience these tools and toys to play with, and helps bring to life the character and the period onstage.

OPPOSITE: *Judi Dench as Irina Nikolayevna Trepleva in* **The Seagull.** *Photo: Robbie Jack*

RIGHT: *A collection of accessories.*

There are hundreds of examples of how large a part accessories play in demonstrating the character of the person who wears or carries them; we are so used to seeing them, that we are scarcely conscious of them. Today, consumers pay extra for desirable designer labels on their accessories, which make them as recognizably expensive as the beautifully etched steel armour of the tournament knight.

This chapter lists a range of accessories in alphabetical order. Books have been written about all these accessories, detailing their appearance and use, and often the etiquette that surrounds them (although the etiquette book for the mobile-phone user is still in flux). The information below gives clues and ideas, but merely skims the surface of a huge subject.

The yellow jacket is defined by the accessories and real-life props.

APRONS

The most basic apron is a bit of cloth tied round the waist. It has been used over hundreds of years to protect clothes from dirt and wear. The blacksmith's apron is thick leather and the young lady at her embroidery might wear an apron no bigger or more substantial than a lace handkerchief. One is essential and practical; the other is a decorative fancy. Aprons are wonderfully useful to the costume designer. They are cheap, easy to make, and provide a splash of colour and a message about the work and class of the wearer. They can cover quite a large percentage of the body without the need for elaborate fitting and they are easy to take on and off. If a character would wear an apron at all, that apron will speak of his class and profession.

BABIES

A prop baby made of an old sweater wrapped up in a blanket can only look convincing if the actor holding it is capable of making the audience believe that a stick of wood is their beloved child. It may be better, for both actor and audience, if the baby is physically more convincing. Even a newborn baby has bulk and weight; its head is round and heavy and its body has a shape that is more than a bundle. A doll of the right size and weight wrapped in a shawl can do the job, provided it is not stiff. A sort of bean-bag roughly shaped like a swaddled child and stuffed with lentils or rice or dried beans may be better; it will be about the right weight for the size and have a slightly squishy quality, which will help its blanketed little body to rest against a shoulder or cuddle up in someone's arms. A pocket at the back of the head will make it possible for the hand of the actor's arm that cradles the baby to make the head move and nuzzle. A baby not wrapped in a blanket is a more difficult proposition as its limbs will show and it will need to be made more like a puppet.

BAGS AND BASKETS

Shopping bags, baskets, sports bags and briefcases all tell us a story about their owners and the times in which they live. People have been weaving baskets with sticks, rushes and grasses since earliest times. It is easy to find modern examples that look as if they come from other eras, although they might have to be broken down a bit with paint or dye. Most women and many men carry a bag when out and about. The women's handbag is a separate subject (*see* page 115), but there are so many other types of bag: shopping bags, of cloth or fabric, sports bags and briefcases; children's satchels of the past and the shoulder bags and haversacks they use today; the doctor's bag of equipment and the lap-top case; the old lady's trundle-trolley and the child's bright plastic lunch-box. Plumbers and diplomats, rat-catchers and violinists – all have to carry the tools of their trades in distinctive bags and cases, which the designer must research and re-create.

BALDRICS, SWORD BELTS AND THE LIKE

Swords have to hang slanting slightly to the back and in a position where they will not trip up the wearer. The guard (the piece that guards the knuckles) on the hilt should face forward. The baldric, or sword belt or, indeed, any other method you use to suspend the sword or its scabbard, must cause the sword to settle at the correct angle. Less sophisticated swords can look as if they are stuck through the belt, although it is wise to make some sort of concealed slot or stiffening to make it easier for the actor to draw and replace the weapon. Clubs, axes, daggers and truncheons may all need some sort of sling or baldric if the actor needs his hands free when he is not wielding them. Belts and baldrics must be strong and substantial. Leather is the best fabric for the job and an old belt can be chopped up and stitched or glued into shape and decorated. You can buy special bladed needles for stitching leather on the machine or by hand, or persuade a cobbler to stitch it for you on his machine. Glue must be strong and reliable; test its reliability viciously before letting it go onstage, to avoid the weapon clanking to the floor at the wrong moment.

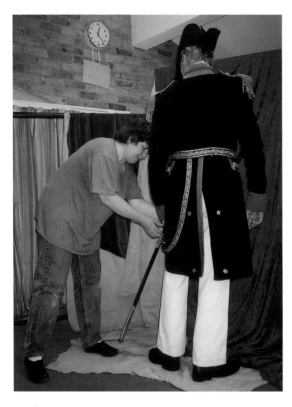

Adjusting a sword-belt. Photo: Robin Cottrell

BELTS

The female waist, as it journeys up and down the body following the dictates of fashion, has often been defined by a belt. Fourteenth-century ladies wore a girdle with the long ends dangling from a knot set low on the hips, to emphasize the long-waisted, slim look that was fashionable at the time; in the 1950s, women wore a tight and often wide belt, to emphasize the hourglass figure that was considered to be desirable during that decade. It is hard to imagine belts and their buckles ever vanishing from women's costume because it is hard to imagine women being disinterested in displaying a fashionable figure. The waist – or, rather, the place fashion chooses as the division between thorax and abdomen – plays such an important part in passing fashion.

Men have always had a more practical attitude to the belt, which has been either a place to house a sword or gun or simply a means to stop trousers falling down. Belt buckles have been as beautiful as jewels for thousands of years and many men would still choose a belt with care and interest. The subtleties of the slight differences in modern men's belts might be lost on stage, but the more obvious styles will be useful to the designer as a visual division between the top and bottom of a body, and a way of keeping folds, pleats and drapes in order.

CANES AND WALKING STICKS

Canes and walking sticks were a part of every fashionable and many working men's outdoor dress until the car became commonplace, and men walked less. Historic paintings show hundreds of examples of men with staffs and sticks and canes. They have been as subject to fashionable development as any other accessory. Their decorative tops and their changing heights are subjects of great interest to collectors and fashion historians. In the time of Charles I, a man would carry a tall cane decorated with tassels; raising his arm to hold this cane displayed the frills and furbelows of the sleeves to greater advantage. In the first half of the nineteenth century, a gentleman would always carry either a cane or an umbrella when walking outdoors. Now, unless people are walking in rough terrain, walking sticks are an aid for the elderly or injured, and have become an eccentric accessory when used by a healthy man.

CRAVATS

Cravats can be the starched white linen that Beau Brummel and his valet spent so many hours perfecting, or the paisley-patterned silk worn by the Country Gentleman in a farce. Cravats are still worn today as a more casual version of the tie, although they tend to be seen on groups of people who continue to favour a rather formal 'country-house' style. Modern cravats are tied in a single loose knot but tying an early nineteenth-century cravat was a skilful business and much advice was published to help the dashing young man about town and his valet to achieve the right fashionable effect. There are plenty of examples between these two extremes; many men tied the cloth around the neck in a more or less appropriate style for the era, and thought no more about it.

DAGGERS AND KNIVES

Daggers are much easier to cope with than swords, both for actors and costumiers. They are easier to keep snugly in place on the belt and can create a decorative touch on a costume. A dagger can look sharp and dangerous and still be beautiful; the size means that a Wardrobe-made dagger can look convincing, as much of it will be covered by the hand when it is in action. There are times when the blade needs to retract into the handle for a convincing stabbing. Prop-hire firms can provide these. Joke shops sell rather feeble-looking versions, but it is possible to make them look more convincing without destroying the mechanism. It works well to wind string or leather thonging round the handle, glueing it as you go to create a more textured surface for painting or decorating. The same method can create a passable flick-knife out of the flick-combs that are available from novelty shops. Make sure that they really are convincing by checking them in the mirror; if you can make them look all right in the Wardrobe, you

can be sure the actor will make a better job of it on stage. All weapons should be checked for safety with the stage manager, who may need to adapt them to make them comply with health and safety regulations.

FANS

The obvious purpose of the fan was originally, and still is in hot countries, to create a cooling draught of air. However, it was also a gentle weapon in the armoury of the flirt, helping her to use her subtle but calculated wiles. It could hide genuine blushes; it could also appear to conceal a low-cut neckline, while its languid flutter drew the imagination to the bosom concealed beneath. Fans developed their own language with which the well-trained user could admonish or seduce.

Fans also provide a splendid canvas for decorative display and they have been painted in the past by great masters. They can be made of ivory and feathers, of rushes and mother-of pearl and paper. Their decorative nature makes them useful to costume designers and their possibilities for wordless play endear them to actresses. It is important to check, when mending or redecorating fans, that they still open and close smoothly. They should also have a loop to slip over the wrist, so that they can dangle gracefully and do

Decorating a belt.

not have to be clutched throughout the performance.

It is also useful to have a sturdy fan in the toolbox to revive an overheated or faint performer at a dress rehearsal; it may be an old-fashioned approach, but it is instant, silent and effective.

FICHUS AND COLLARS

The audience pays more attention to the actor's head, and most particularly his eyes, than to any other part of his body. The neckline of a costume leads the audience to see this all-important head in the best possible aspect and determines how much of the head and shoulders is included in the audience's perception. It seems an obvious observation, but the right ratio of neck to head makes a strong point. The graceful, open neckline of a low bodice draws the eye, first to the bosom (or at least as much of it as can be seen), and then on up to the eyes, which will show why so much is exposed: is it an innocent following of fashion? Is it an invitation to make people want to see more? The high, close-fitting, boned collar of the Edwardian lady accentuates not only the corseted curves below, but also provides a stalk that presents the head and its elaborate hat and hairstyle to the viewer. The tight, starched collar set high on the neck, the collar lying open showing the throat, the soft folds of a cravat, the ruffles or gathers on man's shirt neckline – all tell different stories of periods and personalities. An added, purely pragmatic value on the stage is the possibility of using white near the face, which helps to reflect light on to the actor's expression.

FLOWERS

A bouquet held by a character onstage can be designed as an accessory to the costume. Artificial flowers may decorate hats and costumes and the choice of flowers –daisies, orchids, or whatever – must suit the character in feeling as well as colour. An impressive variety of plastic and cloth flowers can be found. The cheaper ones tend to be mounted on plastic 'stalks', which make them look stiff and unnatural when sewn on a costume. They look softer and more like real flowers if you pull both flowers and leaves off the stalks and rearrange them yourself. You may find a complicated flower like a rose will fall apart when removed from its support, but it can be reassembled and glued on to a small circle of fabric before being attached to the costume.

GLOVES

A glove is a complicated item: a cover for four fingers and a thumb on each hand, all of which are a different size and must be able to bend and grip with precision. According to the story, the King of Spain sent Elizabeth I a pair of gloves that were worth as much as a room in a palace – hardly surprising, when you imagine the skill and work required to create such a subtle structure from unyielding fabric. In the past, ladies would give men gloves as a mark of favour and men would 'throw down the gauntlet' as a challenge to a duel. The debutante of the past would be taught the tricky etiquette of glove-wearing. (Do you wear them at tea when visiting? Could you dance without them? Do you take them off or leave them on if there is a possibility of your hand being kissed?) More recently, bikers' leather gauntlets, children's woolly mittens, Inuit fur and deep-sea divers' polypropylene protect a wide variety of valuable hands from cold and danger.

Gloves give the designer a chance to use an extra splash of colour on one of the most mobile and visible parts of an actor's body, and to tell the audience a story of weather and class and work and sophistication and period. And they can even tell something about age – think of the bright knitted mitts dangling from a string threaded through the young child's sleeve, and the fingerless mittens of the old gardener in the park.

It may be complicated to make a pair of gloves but it is not difficult to alter their appearance once you have a basic glove that is more or less the right colour and texture. Decoration can be added between knuckle and wrist as long as it keeps to the back of the hand. Pale leather and cloth can be painted with dye. Gauntlets can be added to alter the silhouette. False nails or claws can be glued on,

Adding decorated gauntlets to a pair of gloves.

fingers can be cut off to make mittens and UV light-sensitive bones can be painted on a black glove for the scary Hand of the Skeleton.

HAIR DECORATIONS

The way the hair is arranged and dressed is part of the costume design, although the most essential raw material, unless a wig or hat covers the whole head, is the actors' own and a designer has to be inventive to make the best of it. There are times when you will be lucky enough to be working with actors who have the sort of hair that can be arranged in a suitable style; there are other times when nature needs help, and this is when hair decorations can fill the gap. The silhouette of the head reflects the period, and this can be accentuated by feathers, ribbons, flowers or jewels. These little arrangements can be made up in the Wardrobe and stitched or glued on to hair combs or clips that will stay securely anchored in the hair. Long hair, on a short-haired actress, can be suggested with a snood or other net filled with false hair. This will look more convincing if you can find an excuse to make it look as if the net is supposed to show; pearls sewn on gold net, or a thick and clumsy net that is lighter or darker than the actress's own hair will disguise the join between the real hair and the extension.

HANDBAGS

Men's handbags have been, and still are, a practical substitute for a pocket. A woman's handbag is an extension of her personality, and, to judge by literature of the past and women of today, its contents provide telling clues to the life of its owner. The way it is held reflects not only its design, but also the character of the woman. There is the practical stout leather handbag, pressed to the body and held doubly firmly by its leather handles round the arm; the pretty pink bag, swinging through the air like a little pendulum, dangling from the hand of the walking girl; the shoulder bag, practical and commodious on a stout strap, or fashionable and light on its gold chain. An actor will sometimes choose the contents of her handbag for the character she is playing, even though the audience will never see this evidence of her inner stage-life. Handbags onstage must never look empty, no matter what is really inside them, and it helps the actor if they are a believable weight. Check that the clasp or fastening is easy to use and reliable if a bag has to be opened onstage.

HANDKERCHIEFS

There are many stories of a small-part actor upstaging another by playing with a handkerchief and drawing all eyes away from the star of the scene. These stories prove the eye-catching effect of a moving patch of colour on stage; the area of colour may be minute in comparison with the size of a huge auditorium, but it can have the attention-grabbing power of a drum roll. The only time the audience sees a handkerchief, unless it is peeking discreetly from the breast pocket of a man's suit, is when it is being used and moved by the actor. It gives a design opportunity for a strong little moment that will say something about the character. It might seem a lot of fuss about a detail, but imagine a small orange silk handkerchief being produced to mop tears at a funeral, or a pauper pulling a white lace and lawn square from her rags.

MOBILE PHONES, I-PODS

Items of modern technology need to look appropriate because they are so recognizable to today's audience, or at least to some of them. And they change so rapidly. Few people will know if a fan is years out of date or a sword hilt is a little out of fashion, but many of the audience will notice a three-year-old mobile phone in the hands of a young, urbane character. They are as much a badge of today's century as swords were in an earlier one. They can affect the way people stand and walk when they are using them in as idiosyncratic a manner as a weapon or a broom or a crutch. A modern crowd coming out of a building behaves in a way that could belong to no other century, as they switch on, talk and check or send text messages.

JEWELLERY

All jewellery that can be seen on stage will be noticed by the audience. Even something as small

A heap of jewellery to pick through at a car-boot sale.

as a nose-stud will flash a glinting ray of light to the back row of the gallery. The hard, shiny surface of metal and jewels reflects all the light that falls on it. Consequently, it is important to use the right jewellery on the right characters. At least, it has to look right; it does not have to *be* right. Many actresses have a collection of costume jewellery that they will be happy to let the designer choose from. Glue and beads can transform plain stud earrings into long dangling ones. Necklaces and bracelets can be made from combinations of braid and beads and fastened with tiny strips of Velcro or a hook and eye or press stud. 'Diamonds' and 'pearls' can be bought by the metre and transformed into sparkling and sophisticated parures. Tiaras can be constructed on hairbands and ethnic jewellery made from painted bamboo, leather and beads, or even plastic tubing. Any car-boot sale will have a stallholder selling a tangled heap of broken necklaces, brooches and watches that can be transformed into an Aladdin's cave of treasure – as long as nobody looks too closely.

MEDALS

Medals are a problem. It can take extensive research to track down exactly which medals would have been worn by military characters in a play, and a long time to re-create them, but the hire charges of replica medals may be beyond the reach of a small company. Army museums are particularly helpful in the search for correct information. There may be only one person in the audience who recognizes a mistake but that mistake will be glaring to that person, and destroy his belief in the character. A medium- or high-ranking soldier must have his medals if he is to convince the audience of his rank. It is better to suggest the costume and its insignia with a representative uniform than to make an inaccurate attempt to create the real thing.

MUFFS

The muff, a warm tube of cloth or fur that was usually suspended on a cord or gold or silver chain round the neck, has vanished from the modern wardrobe. Although it was essentially a feminine accessory, in the seventeenth- and eighteenth-century days of peacock costume, men, too, could be seen pacing in the park with their hands in a muff. Muffs ranged in size from being 'big enough for a harlequin to jump through' to a tiny little ball of fur just large enough to hold two small hands, and perhaps a purse. They can be a pretty and evocative way of suggesting cold weather on stage.

PARASOLS

Parasols were a vital accessory at the time when it was the mark of a lady to have a fair skin; only a manual worker would have been out in the sunshine, and the coarsening effect of weather on skin was a danger to those who aspired to a delicate and youthful beauty. Before the development of sunscreen lotions, parasols and gloves were used to protect uncovered skin. It is not hard to bodge together a parasol that does not have to be opened. It becomes more difficult if the character must be seen walking, parasol open in the garden. Torn parasols, or small old-fashioned umbrellas, can be found cheaply in junk shops and sales; check that the spines are unbroken and that you can make the parasol frame open and shut. It is not as difficult as you might think to re-cover them if they have one untorn section for you to copy. Be exact with your pattern and the seam allowances; any slight variation, when multiplied by the number of segments in the parasol, may jam the opening

mechanism. Refurbish the stick and make and decorate the whole cover before you attach it to the frame.

PURSES AND POUCHES

Small, modern purses have little importance onstage as they are usually concealed in the actor's hand. However, the purses of our ancestors are more important to the costume designer, as they can be as much a punctuation mark in the costume as a pair of gloves or a collar. Men wore them strung on their belts to keep their money safe, in the days when tunics and doublets were more common than trousers, and opportunistic thieves were known as 'cut-purses' rather than 'pick-pockets'. The purses might be jewelled pouches full of golden coins or a scrubby bit of leather held together with twine and containing a bit of bread and an onion – the silk purse and the sow's ear. They have never gone out of fashion, although, as paper money and pockets have developed, men have moved to wallets and women, more aware of the lumpy outline loose change gives in a pocket, have kept the purse. How often in plays is the purse of money put on the table, the gold handed to the hit-man by the villain, and the coin given to the servant? The actor takes the money from the purse on his belt if he is wearing pocketless tights. Women have always used purses but their skirts allow for pockets and they have kept their purses in handbags of sorts for a couple of hundred years. Once again, pouches, after a gap of five hundred years, are back on men's belts – as a safe house for a camera or a mobile phone.

RINGS

Rings are so small, compared with the huge area onstage, that it's easy to imagine the audience would not notice them. But they encircle fingers that are used by actors to emphasize their words with gesture. Rings are always hard and reflective, and, even if the audience cannot distinguish the colour of a gem, they will certainly see it flash. Inexperienced actors may need to be reminded to remove their own rings if they are not appropriate.

There will always be someone in the audience who will notice when a wedding ring has been forgotten. Some people have a strong-rooted fear that it is unlucky to take off a wedding ring; in such cases, the ring can be covered with a narrow strip of sticking plaster or masking tape, which can be made up to match the skin. Plain rings can be bought from bead shops and have a flat section that allows you to stick on a suitable jewel.

ROSETTES

A rosette is a circle of gathered cloth and can provide a useful splash of colour or decoration. Rosettes can be worn on a neck ribbon round an eighteenth-century woman's neck and can decorate sashes and necklines in the same way as jewels. They can also be useful, when appropriate to the period, to cover up the shortcomings of a shoe that is not really in period. Rosettes of ribbon and cloth are easy and cheap to make from scraps of fabric, and can be useful to the designer when she wants a more definite splash of colour than a jewel would provide. Take half a metre (a couple of feet) of 25-mm (1-in) wide ribbon, join it in a circle, run a gathering thread along one long edge and pull it up tightly, then flatten it and settle it with the steam iron. Once you have made one it will become clear how to vary it if you want to

Two types of ruffle: a circular cut one on the outer frill and a straight gathered one on the inner frill.

make it larger or smaller, or more layered and decorative. A pasting with PVA glue will stiffen it; although the glue will whiten the fabric when wet, it will dry clear.

RUCKSACKS AND HAVERSACKS

A strange ritual became commonplace in the 1980s. Two friends or lovers walk along, apparently engaged in an amicable conversation. They stop, suddenly. One turns their back on the other for a short pause and then they continue to walk as before. It would have seemed, to an onlooker from the past, like a courtship ritual as strange as that of the peacock; in fact, one was extracting an object from the other's rucksack. The haversack has evolved from the luggage system for the traveller without a porter to a fashion item and has, in many cases, replaced the handbag for women. The bent silhouette with the huge growth on its back remains, however, the badge of the student traveller.

RUFFLES

Ruffles flutter and flop on male and female costume through many centuries and in a huge variety of shapes and colours and fabrics. There are the muslin frills, scarcely thicker than a mist of white, which pretend to conceal the bosom revealed by a low-cut bodice. There are crisp layered ruffles, which give a jagged edge to the silhouette of a skirt. Some men may wear a double row of ruffles down the front of a dress shirt and the Caroline courtier might have yards of lace and silk drooping and flowing from his sleeves. All these ruffles are produced from two basic methods – the straight gathered strip or the cut circle.

RUFFS

It is difficult to suggest late sixteenth- and early seventeenth-century costume without the ruff. It has such a powerful silhouette and the way it presents the head on a sort of plate of starched cloth is unforgettable. Ruffs take a long time to make and are difficult to launder, and it is a blessing for the costume designer that the humbler workers in the play will not be wearing them. That complicated, starched white neckwear was a sign in the past that you had enough servants to keep you supplied with freshly laundered linen.

SASHES

A strip of cloth wound round the waist, or crossing the chest from shoulder to waist, a sash is really a simple belt, but it has extra possibilities. The cloth can be quite wide and, once it has been wound round and tied with the ends hanging at the hip, a significant proportion of the actor's costume is covered by its colour. The simplest tunic can be made to look exotic or grand with the addition of a gorgeous strip of cloth. The sash calls for no careful cutting and any flaws in the fabric can be disguised with a bit of twist and drape.

European men's fashion left sashes behind around two hundred years ago, although upper-class children like Little Lord Fauntleroy still wore them in the nineteenth and very early twentieth century. Military dress uniforms still include them today and they have always been part of folk and national dress. Sashes still crop up occasionally in women's and girls' ball gowns and party dresses. Eighteenth-century portraits, particularly the pastoral ones, show a lot of sash draping going on, but the hey-day of the sash was the nineteenth century. The white lawn, silk and muslin dresses, which were the rule for most girls and young woman when they dressed in their best, were enlivened by the band of colour at the waist. There are many autobiographical records of the delight of these girls in the gift of a new silk sash.

SCARVES

The scarf, a square, rectangular or triangular piece of cloth, gives the designer another quick and definite patch of colour that can change the look of an actor or a costume. Women have used head-scarves to cover their heads for as long as they have woven cloth. The scarf can be tied at the back, in gypsy fashion, which conceals much of the hair and creates a neat round silhouette. Tied under the chin, it gives the face a more triangular shape; wound round the head and neck, it produces the soft outline that recalls Biblical times. It is possible, using the scarf as a sort of frame, to change the look of an actress quite dramatically, as the scarf can be arranged to alter the relative proportions of the face and neck; as such, it is particularly useful when an actress is doubling roles. Scarves can hide the neck, which is one of the most obvious pointers to youth when a young actress is playing an older woman.

The bias edge of the fabric (the long edge of the triangle if you fold a square from corner to corner) is the edge that should frame the face. Bias fabric has a natural stretch and the scarf will lie snugly against the skin. A small comb can be stitched to the underside of the cloth to stop the tied scarf slipping forward or back.

Long woollen scarves are sometimes used as insignia by schools, colleges and clubs. The traditional college scarf is made up of strips of college colours sewn into lengthwise stripes. The school scarf is more likely to be knitted in widthwise stripes of the school colours. Mothers used to cross their small children's scarves over the chest and tie them at the back to protect them on the chilly walk to school, and still do in colder countries. Boys and medieval man tucked the end of a scarf made of double fabric and wore it on the head like a beanie hat with a tail wound round the neck. A bohemian Victorian or Edwardian man might wind an extra-long scarf twice around the neck with both ends dangling almost to the floor. Lighter neck scarves have never been out of fashion – they are so useful to women, as a colourful and elegant addition to their dress. That splash of colour or emphasis to the line of a costume can be so easily achieved with a scarf and is as useful to theatre designers as to women and men in everyday life.

SHAWLS

A shawl may be thick and woollen, or made of silk, with tassels. Shawls come ragged or sequinned or plaid, and in lightest, thinnest wool, so fine you can almost see through it. Shawls wrap babies and

119

beggars and ladies and lairds – Macbeth's tartan plaid is, like it or not, a manly shawl. In the past, a shawl was a desirable possession, with adventurous men coming home from their travels bringing exotic examples for their wives and sisters and lovers. These beautiful textiles, rich in colour and embroidery, were a far cry from the old sack cut open at the seam and used to keep the rain off the fishwives at the harbour.

A shawl is a flat piece of cloth. It can be triangular or rectangular or square. It can be less than a square metre or big enough to cover a grand piano, plain or patterned, fringed or straight-edged. What could be more simple, more variable or easier to make? It is not, however, so easy to wear with any elegance. It is not hard if you are playing a fishwife or the old biddy on the doorstep, but it takes practice to sweep about the stage as a sophisticated and fashionable Victorian as if you have no trouble coping with those yards of fringed and slippery cloth. The knack involves draping the shawl so that the weight is supported and kept in place by the position of the forearms held with the elbows bent.

SHOES

Actors will check their appearance in mirrors at fittings, in the dressing rooms and before they go onstage, to make sure they can imagine the way they will look to the audience. When they leave the mirror, the feeling of the character they saw reflected in the glass stays with them; one of powerful reminders of that feeling is the way they move as the character, and the way they move becomes connected with the shoes they are wearing. Shoes should look appropriate to the period and character, and be comfortable and suitable for all the movement that occurs on the stage. But it is equally important that they feel right to the actor's creation of his character. Shoes alter the way people walk. It is impossible to wear trainers and feel and walk like an Edwardian, and difficult to play a child when wearing high-heeled shoes. Boots, slippers, dance pumps or court shoes all engender a different gait. It helps actors if they can have the shoes they will wear in performance

Adapted footwear: a boot with fabric top and old belt strap; a painted shoe; a dyed shoe; Wellingtons with glitter glue; and a re-cut lace-up shoe with the tongue worn on the outside to conceal the laces.

early enough to use them in rehearsal. The designer can tell if they look right, but only the actor will know if they help him or her to breathe life into a role.

SPECTACLES, LORGNETTES AND MONOCLES

Spectacles can change the shape of a face. Consequently, they can be used as a quick-change disguise where an actor is doubling roles, and can help to age a young actor playing an older role; they blur the outline of the eyebrow, which throws a distinctive shadow on the upper face and is one of the most recognizable features of an actor onstage. The way people look through their spectacles is distinctive. They lower their chin and raise their eyebrows to look over their half-moon glasses or gaze more owlishly through large round ones. Thick black rims, thin gold ones, outrageous diamante wing-shaped frames, all add to the audience's perception of the character. The Lady Bracknell-style lorgnette is hand-held in front of the eyes on a stick. The monocle is a single eyeglass usually worn on a narrow black cord round the neck. When needed, it is kept in place in front of the eye by a contraction of the eyebrow and cheek muscles, giving the face a slightly lopsided look.

The theatrical business with glasses is useful to actors: they can take the glasses on and off to emphasize a pause, polish them and point with them, and slide them up and down their nose. Dark glasses and sunglasses are an instant mask for the features. Mirrored sunglasses that reflect the light back to the audience can have a particularly sinister effect onstage. Different shapes and styles of spectacles belong to different times and can help to set a period as well as character. An optician can replace the prescription lenses in glasses with clear glass for stage use. As the light can reflect on the glass, and make it difficult for the audience to catch an actor's expression, it can be better if the glass is removed completely. The easiest way to do this is to wrap the glasses in a cloth and whack the lens through the cloth with a hammer. You will need to be absolutely meticulous in making sure the frame is checked for smoothness, but the glass usually breaks cleanly and crisply and drops out into the cloth.

SUITCASES AND OTHER LUGGAGE

Luggage changes with the times. A hundred years ago, the less affluent traveller would take a case made of nothing more substantial than cardboard, or bundles and baskets that they could carry themselves, holding their few belongings. Reasonably well-off travellers, however, packed leather suitcases, which were then adorned with brightly coloured labels from the countries they visited, as well as from trains, hotels or boats. A gentleman might take a trunk as big as a small wardrobe, to carry the huge amount of clothes necessary for someone who had to change for lunch and dinner and the theatre, not to mention the hunting and shooting involved in a country-house weekend. His wife would take just as much, although not as much as her grandmothers and grandfathers. Lord Byron (who else?) was reputed to have had his carriage dismantled and carried piece by piece over the Alps, with quite a large selection from his library, and probably quite a lot of clothes as well. Everything would have been carried by porters or servants.

Porters with piles of cases on trolleys used to be as much a part of the scene at railway stations and docks as the passengers. But new, more easily washable fabrics and more casual clothes meant much lighter and smaller luggage. As bags and cases became more manageable, the porters began to disappear. The modern traveller does his own portering, trundling a neat little case around on its own wheels.

It is possible to find pictures and photographs of men and women on journeys relating to every period and it is important to get the luggage right. Images of travel are so familiar from films and documentaries that a pile of luggage on a station platform, and the silhouette of its owner, can set a period for the audience. A figure in a shawl with a pile of baskets and bundles tells a different story from a top-hatted and walking-sticked gent with his trunks and suitcases.

SWORDS

Swords have a two-edged purpose in men's costume. They were necessary as a means of self-defence in times past, when men had to be prepared to protect themselves and their loved ones from sudden danger. They were also, like all kinds of weapons, a fashionable accessory, and a status symbol to their male owners. Blood channels in the blade and the decoration of the hilt were the subject of as much interest to men of the past as the latest technology is today – a heady combination of practicality and power. King Arthur's heavy and magical Excalibur and Cyrano de Bergerac's witty, supple blade are extreme examples of swords – one of a style so heavy that its use could require two strong arms to cleave an armoured skull; the other, precise, light and pin-point deadly. If you give even the most modern and mild actor a sword at a fitting, you will see an instant change in his posture and gaze.

TIES

Ties have evolved from a bow of ribbon round the neck into a high-fashion object. As men's business suits have become more conventional and monochrome, the tie has been allowed to express personality with colour and pattern. The correct knot and width are decreed by the fashion, although most men continue to wear the knot they used when they wore their first adult suit. The designer and the actor can enjoy discovering the perfect tie for a character.

TOYS

Toys are not strictly within the remit of the costume department but, when adults are playing children, the toy they carry becomes almost part of the costume. This is particularly the case with dolls. The doll has to be dressed in a style that is appropriate to the class and period of the child who owns it, and the costume department can be the best place to make a good job of it. The same is true of most soft toys and the more toy-like puppets.

UMBRELLAS

Umbrellas come in a number of marvellous shapes, from the small and nearly flat to the huge half-sphere. It is so useful in a theatrical context that they take up so little room when closed and so much room when opened; forty black umbrellas can be stored in a dustbin-sized container in the wings but they can fill a whole stage when they are carried on in the funeral procession. Umbrellas have to be used with care by actors. It is easy for the light to be kept off the face and easy to forget how much space is occupied by a person with an umbrella. Umbrella scenes must be carefully choreographed.

Some older umbrellas have a distinctive and beautiful shape and it is worth repairing or re-covering them, provided the frame is strong enough. If they are difficult to open and shut, it may be that the spokes have rusted slightly, which causes the joints to stick instead of slide. Rub them with emery paper and finish with a rag soaked in light oil until they run smoothly.

VEILS

The audience can see quite well through fabrics that appear solid onstage as long as the light hits the cloth from the front. The powerful stage light shining from behind will cause many fabrics to appear almost transparent and show the silhouette of the body clearly beneath the clothes. The darker the fabric, the more solid it will appear. For occasions when the audience needs to see the actor's expression through the veil, the widest mesh possible should be used and the effect checked in the correct lighting from every part of the auditorium. A spotted net veil may look elegant and sophisticated in the Wardrobe, but onstage it could replicate a severe case of acne, or be impenetrable to the audience's eyes.

WATCHES

Watches – wrist and fob – often crop up in the costume plot, and even when they are not mentioned they are a useful accessory that fleshes out the costume in a naturalistic play. They look oddly out of place in any performance that has the slightest abstract nature; a wrist-watch in a dance piece would jar unless its meaning was pointed by the action. The watch chain that attaches the pocket watch to the waistcoat is a useful design accessory, as it glints in the light and adds interest to a dark suit. Watches, of course, are as subject to changes of fashion as any other accessory. Wrist-watches were rare before the 1930s; before that time, a woman would have been more likely to use a watch rather like a brooch – a more glamorous version of the nurse's watch – while a man would have worn a waistcoat, in which he would have kept a pocket watch. A watch was an expensive item until the middle of the twentieth century and it was unusual for children or poor people to own one.

Actors work to a strict time schedule and are used to wearing a wrist-watch, so they may need to be reminded to take it off for the performance.

OPPOSITE: **Martyn Jacques and Julian Bleach in Shockheaded Peter.** *Photo: Robbie Jack*

10 INVENTION IN THE REHEARSAL ROOM

Costume design and making is a changeable job. There has always been a blurred line between costumes and props – the phrase 'costume prop' used to be understood to cover handbags and handkerchiefs, scarves and walking sticks, and still is in many theatre productions – but, with the growth of companies that develop their work through rehearsal, the designer may now be found participating in the inventive work of the rehearsal room, particularly when the script is devised. In addition, she may be required to design much more than just clothes. Props, puppets, masks and magic may be included in her design brief. In these cases, she will be employed as much for her invention in the rehearsal room as for her practical design ability and experience. The genre of work that uses designers as generators, rather than dressers, of ideas has influenced many directors, and has opened up and expanded the job of costume design. It may seem a new development, but director/writer/designer partnerships have been around for hundreds of years. The design-led, post-modern performances of today would not have seemed strange to a Christmas company in Victorian times in London's Drury Lane or Covent Garden – although the content might have been rather surprising.

This type of participation in productions alters the job of costume design in a vital way. The usual solitary study of the script, well-defined research and quiet hours in the studio vanish. The designer is flung into a rehearsal room jangling with ideas and conflicting egos, and is included in the process of refining and sorting, through a mixture of mutual invention and communication, an exciting, overgrown jungle of ideas into a pattern that will include the audience.

DESIGNING FOR DEVISED WORK

Before the first rehearsal, the concept of the production will be discussed at various meetings. A professional company will have a wide-based but secure structure on which to build; this structure will have been set in place in order to arrange funding for the project. An amateur or student company will have a less urgent need to create a structure before the start of rehearsals; salaries, and many of the production expenses incurred by professional groups do not apply, and their audience numbers are more assured. This may prove a two-edged sword to the company as well as to the designer. Huge tracts of time (during which any costume decision is impossible), may be spent in experimentation, and it may transpire that none of the results of these activities have any application to the final performance.

Workshops

Many devising companies run a workshop or series of workshops before the concentrated work of rehearsal begins. The workshop may include the design team – designers of sound and lighting as well as of costume and set – and producers, directors, choreographers and performers. Or it may be a simple matter of a group with an idea meeting together to explore possibilities. It can bring an extra dimension to the inventive scope of the workshop to have a designer present. There is always a danger of the ideas, which come from every member of the company, becoming wildly impracticable. Alternatively, they may exist clear and sharp in the mind of their creator but be seen in a different light by the rest of the company. A designer can help make a misty notion more concrete, either by drawing or by suggesting an object, prop or costume, which helps bring the idea out of the fog and into the light. In order to do this, the designer must come prepared.

Preparing for a Workshop

The first step for the designer is to research the subject and the company. Previous work by the group or the director will give a good guide to the form that the workshop will take. A workshop with a company that works from a very physical, movement-led base will not necessarily use the same stimuli as a company that is creating a script-led project on a historical subject. A company that wants to create a show including puppets and magic may need more practical equipment with which to experiment than a company which plans an interactive community project. A well-prepared table of stimuli can make a huge contribution to the success of the workshop days. The costume designer may assemble a table that she hopes will be particularly inspiring for costume, but the company will and should use it for any idea that occurs. Everything, including ideas, in the devising workshop belongs to everybody.

Below are some tried and tested suggestions:

- *Paper* – drawing paper, newspaper, cling film, wrapping paper, wallpaper, bubble wrap, any sort of paper as long as it is cheap and plentiful. It can be used for drawing on, for scrunching into bundles, for its sound, for stuffing into clothes to alter body shapes, to define areas in the rehearsal room or perhaps as the germ of an idea for a puppet flight of birds wheeling and swooping over a shipwrecked sailor. Or even to read. Cling-film can create a corset, a wall or a waterfall.
- *Sticks* – to walk with, to carry, to raise things higher than hands can, to knock and drum, to be weapons or farm tools or horses or houses.
- *Cloth* – lycra or any other strong, stretchy,

resilient cloth is excellent. It can be wound round a body without slipping or impeding movement and can be cut without fraying. It can bandage, mask and blindfold. It can be a prison or a ghost or a mountain side or a shroud. Bodies and boxes can alter its shape. A slit in it can expand to a birth canal and a man can drown in the sucking bog of a tube of it. It may have wonderful propensities for imaginative play but it is also good practical stuff, which washes, does not crease, is tough as old boots and can be mended over and over again with a zigzag stitch on the sewing machine.
- *String, rope, elastic in long lengths and rubber bands* – apart from their obvious uses, rope and elastic have a way of enticing ideas from people and encouraging actors to work as a group. You will see something beginning to grow as soon as two actors take hold of the two ends of a rope or one actor draws a pattern on the ground with its coils, or when three or four performers begin to work within an enclosing circle of elastic.
- *Sticky tape* – gaffer tape (also known as duck-tape), sellotape and masking tape. For once, the cheapest you can find will be the best for the purpose as it will make it easier to unstick everything and clear up afterwards. It can stick the crumpled head of newspaper on the pole to make a life-sized temporary puppet, or attach paper or cloth to bodies or objects as a suggestion of costume or set.
- *Tools* – scissors, stapler, safety pins, drawing pins, blue-tack, pliers. You will need your own sketch book and pencil to demonstrate graphically what the stick with various lumps of paper and tatters of cloth stuck on to might look like when refined, in the workroom, into Prospero's cloak, staff, book and cave.
- *Hats* – certain hats may be suggested by the subject matter: tin hats for war, scarves for refugees, bowlers, bonnets and top hats to suggest the past. But the most useful may be a supply of cheap baseball caps, which can stand in for any type of headgear until the real thing arrives at a later stage of rehearsal.

It may seem unlikely that this clutch of stuff, which is so close to the makeshift toys and the dressing-up box that have always stirred the imagination of children, can have such a powerful and releasing effect on the imagination of experienced, adult performers. However, you will find that such a box of tricks works time after time – too often to count as a lucky coincidence.

The nature of the project may influence your preparations. You might feel that it would be a particular help to have a heavy greatcoat available for one project, and a huge, filmy cloak or a puppet child for another. However, as a general rule, the things you bring should provide food for the imagination rather than specific information for the performer. The unfinished and gimcrack nature of the stimuli leaves everyone free to re-invent without feeling tied down by the complete and literal nature of the objects they are playing with.

Seeing and working with actors playing with and creating ideas leads to a much more lively interaction between designer and director and performer – and this interplay is essential to the development from workshop to performance.

After the Workshop

The workshopping period has come to an end. Everything is cleared away and the company disbanded for perhaps the weekend, the month or even a year. It is time to make sure that, even if a long time should pass before the project comes to fruition, the hard work will not be forgotten and wasted. There may be a file of notes, a full sketch book, photos and videos. There will also be all the ideas and thoughts and pictures in your head. These are bright and crisp just after the workshop's end, but are soon nudged aside and smudged by new events and experience. It is most important to write down and draw everything you have seen while it is fresh, and make notes that will enable you to remember and replay in your imagination at a later date all the useful information. It can be a great help to have a company meeting soon after the workshop period to exchange reactions to the work that was achieved, and to talk about its future progress.

The style of the costumes you will design will have been conceived during those messy, fragmented hours of sticking and rummaging. You have seen how the actors move and react to their costume and props. You have watched how, with the bits of cloth and gaffer tape and sticks, they use the train of a skirt or the weight of a baby or the brutal strength of a rifle in the development of characterizations. The real costumes and props that you develop will reflect that knowledge and will give, if you are lucky, a support and inspiration to the actor in their performance that they could get in no other way. And the audience will catch their belief.

Designing and Creating Costumes During Rehearsal

The time available to make or find the costumes for a devised piece may be very short, particularly when the designer is also the maker and shopper. It is essential to spend as much time as possible in the rehearsal room, but equally essential that the ideas produced in these sessions come to fruition. One way to cope with this anomaly is to design a basic costume in collusion with the company, or with the director, if the company is not assembled. This can be made, and shoes found and fitted, before rehearsals start. The discipline of having the basic costume in place, and the actors having a clear visual picture of their appearance, will make the business of creating ideas more clear-cut. The whole company will start with the same picture of the way they will look as a group, and their ideas, your ideas and the director's ideas are much more likely to coincide. The accessories and additions that the company decides to make to the costumes during the process of rehearsal will be influenced by the basic costume.

The practical advantage to the designer/maker is that much of the time-swallowing work has been done in advance. The shopping, the shoes, the fittings and subsequent alterations and finishing can be completed as soon as the actors are cast and before rehearsals begin. This leaves more time to

OPPOSITE: **The basic costume of a blouse and skirt is altered with additional garments.**

Bright Angel '98.
Hillary

as mother
in
basic

hat to go out
with coat
as Ms Walter

Fran
Wolf

Ms Walter
(with specs?)

coat & flower
for wedding

coat knit and
for interview

coat back to front
for priest or
with Cape if
needed.

Hillary's   shared
blouse   coat black/grey.
skirt   scarf.
Stockings   Poss. overall
Shoes.   "   hat.

spend in rehearsal, in discussion and in experiment; if the preparatory work happens before rehearsals, there should enough time to develop the new ideas.

The Designer in Rehearsal

It can be expensive to have a professional costume designer who attends rehearsals on a regular basis. It can also be difficult to arrange in companies that are not based in a building where the whole company works in close proximity. Some designers do not enjoy working in an environment where decisions become more public. They may find themselves distracted and annoyed by the demands of the daily dialogue that a good working relationship with the actors necessitates. They may find it difficult to accept that the ideas the company produce must be considered and may be absorbed into the design of the costumes. The designer has less control over the process, often creating a balance of random ideas instead of developing those he has instigated. It becomes more difficult to create a perfect picture and much time has to be given to establishing a relationship of trust with the actor.

Despite these extra rocks in the pathway, there is no doubt that the actor feels more confident in a costume that is the result of collaboration. The design of the costume will have been influenced by *his* body and *his* characterization. Much of the understanding of each character's physical and mental life will arrive, not so much from words, as from an observation of the growth of the character created throughout rehearsal. The ideas embodied in the design will help the actor move as easily and naturally as he does in his own clothes. The notes that the director and choreographer give to the performers, and the discussions that take place at all stages of the process, will include the designer and their content will seep into the designs. The costumes will grow as organically as the performances through this creative exchange and add to their strength. Apart from all the serious stuff, the director will have an easier time if the actors are happy with their costumes and props; she will be able to spend less time solving practical problems and more time actually directing.

LARGE-SCALE SCHOOL AND COMMUNITY PROJECTS

Amateur or community groups may employ a professional designer to create the costumes for their performance. You can plan and plot these unwieldy projects. You can sit at a drawing board or a computer and work out exactly what you would like the project to look like and exactly what each character should wear. But, unless you have a huge pot of money and a lot of efficient assistance, your concept is likely to begin to fall apart when it makes the transition from drawing board to reality. You must work with the cast, in rehearsal and at meetings, to make sure that they understand and will support your idea.

Presenting Your Ideas

Many of the cast in such a project will be inexperienced performers, without the driving ambition and serious work intentions of the professional actor. They may have little or no conception of the importance you attach to the picture that the audience will see. They have no particular reason to trust your ideas rather than their own, and may not see any difference between dressing up for their own fun and pleasure, and putting on a costume to help the audience to a greater understanding of the performance. And why should they? They are joining in the project out of a love of performing and to have a good time, and that enjoyment often shines out in the exuberance of the performance. The fact that they are not professional actors, with the anxieties and pre-conceived ideas that can develop through training and experience, and are performing for the sheer enjoyment of it, can give the designer a wonderful opportunity for imaginative and innovative work. The cast and their relatives will amaze and inspire you with their generous and practical support – once they know what you are trying to do. It is always worth taking time to present your ideas clearly.

The actors, even the youngest child on the stage, will understand a costume design, as long as it is presented in the right way. You can talk until you are blue in the face about basic costume or design concept or period detail and achieve nothing, but a drawing will do it for you in a few seconds. Show the designs, perhaps at the first meeting of the company. Explain which parts of the costume you hope the actors will provide themselves, and which parts you will provide, or must be made. Ask for helpers and volunteers. Find out the people in the company who can sew or paint or dye or glue. Show an example of the way you imagine the angels' haloes and wings to look and arrange a workshop day when you and your helpers can make twenty haloes, or thirty or even a hundred; it might take one person five days to make a batch of masks, but it will take five workers one day. Adjust your ideas to the skill of your helpers; a simple design that works every time will create a better effect onstage than a more elaborate one that is outside the practical abilities of the workers.

It is a different skill to design for these sort of projects. You must use simple, clear effects that can be easily achieved, and create the drama of the designs through the way you group the colours and textures onstage.

Achieving a Coherent Picture

The main difficulty experienced by the costume designer working on large-scale or community projects where actors provide many of their own clothes, comes in creating a coherent picture. Helpful performers or their mothers may spend much time and money creating a costume that seems right for their character, but is much too elaborate for the scheme you have planned; others may provide nothing at all. You have to be tactful and adaptable or you will forfeit the goodwill of some of the company. But you also have to give value to the people who are employing you, and to the audience who will see the production. The clearer you make your concept to everyone at the start of the project, and throughout rehearsals, the more likely you are to end up with a good result at the first night.

It is difficult to succeed in creating this sort of work from a distance unless you work with a tried and tested costume supervisor, whom you can trust to adapt your designs in a way that you will approve. You need to be around to answer questions and prevent people wasting time making things that will not be used, and to encourage and organize the creation of useful costumes. You need to be on the spot to make changes when an idea becomes impracticable and has to be adjusted, and you need to be ready to prevent a good idea being chucked away because it does not work first time. You also need to be there to control the budget and make sure, particularly if the project takes place over a long time span, that the realization of the costumes moves steadily forward.

Sharing Skills and Ideas

Dyeing a Set of Costumes

Ask everyone to bring in old cotton clothes that they no longer want. Show them how to look at the manufacturer's label (sometimes concealed in the side seam rather than placed obviously in the centre-back), in order to check that they contain a high percentage of cotton. Explain that polyester, nylon and some other man-made cloth is more difficult to dye. Show an example of a patterned cloth on a white background that you have dyed a colour, so that the pattern now shows on a coloured ground. Arrange to collect the clothes at a group rehearsal. You may find that you have to buy a few extra garments to have enough for everyone in the scene you are planning. Dye, or ask one of your volunteers to dye, the whole lot together in the colour or colours you have chosen. In this way you will have created, with a minimum of fuss and expense, a picture that is the result of many people's input but is coherent with your design.

Adapting a Basic Costume

It can be difficult to explain to inexperienced actors how a simple addition to a basic costume can give the audience an impression of different characters. It is easier to get the message across by demonstration. Ask someone in a black top and skirt to put on, perhaps, a feather boa and a pair of elbow-length gloves and then to change them for an apron and a headscarf. Once the members of the company understand that you are aiming for a design concept that uses such simple but

129

Neck can be a gap in the stitching (closed with press studs) or a slit in the front.

Sleeve and body shape can be altered by simple changes to the cutting lines.

Cutting line

An extremely simple, easily adaptable pattern.

informative accessories, they can begin to choose and assemble items with your advice. It will soon become clear to them that you do not need a complete, naturalistic costume to give the message to the audience.

Inventing an Adjustable Pattern

There will be occasions when a set of costumes may be farmed out to many different people. The costumes have to look the same onstage but may have to be made in various sizes, by a number of different people with different levels of skill. Two factors make this a viable possibility: the pattern should be simple and the fabric should be provided. A limited budget may make it necessary for everyone to pay for their own materials, but at least they will be buying the fabric the designer has chosen. The fabric is likely to cost less when bought in quantity and chosen with a regard to price as well as design.

The pattern must be as straightforward as can be managed and the amount of cloth worked out via a ratio of the performer's measurements. The angel's robe is a useful example. It is a standard medieval shape – an elongated 'T'. The measurement of a length can be established by measuring the actor from neck to ground. The number of lengths required can be calculated by asking the performer to stretch out his arms like a cross and taking the measurement from thumb to thumb. This measurement is an excellent guide to the size of the actor. A ground-length robe for an actor where this measurement is the same or less than the width of the material will use double the measurement of cloth; a measurement that is more than the length will use four times the length of cloth. In both cases, this will allow sufficient fabric for the wings of all these different-sized angels (or for sashes and hat trimmings if they are not angels, but characters appearing in a medieval court or Sinbad's marketplace).

The pattern should be a diagram with a series of easy-to-follow drawings and instructions. It is not necessary to make a paper pattern if the instructions are clear. It will make it a great deal easier for the makers if they can see and examine a finished garment and perhaps watch a demonstration cutting session. Many people whose sewing is quite good enough for theatrical purposes are nervous about cutting. It may be easier to get volunteers if you arrange for one or two people to collect all the measurements and do all the cutting, and then pass the job on to others for sewing.

11 PRODUCTION WEEK

The last week of preparation arrives. However long or short the rehearsal time has been, the moment when everything you have been working on must be completed begins to rush towards you. Every aspect of the production must be ready for the first-night audience and every single person involved in the production, from ticket seller to leading actor, is infected with deadline tension. Very few people work in theatres for disinterested financial gain; most, front-of-house as well as backstage, have an urgent interest in the work and a corresponding emotional drive geared towards the success of a production. The combined nervous tension in all these people makes the last few days of rehearsal particularly demanding and exciting. The costume department prepares for the whirlwind hour when the company of actors will all dress in their completed costumes for the first time.

THE TECHNICAL REHEARSAL

The technical rehearsal, or 'tech', may go on for several days. Every technical aspect of the show is rehearsed, checked and re-worked until all problems have been solved. Every scene and costume change, the lighting and sound states, special effects and all the cues and quick changes must be tested. The actors work slowly through the play with the director and crew.

The plot calls for the audience to see Peter Pan flying in through the window. In rehearsal,

*OPPOSITE: **Laura Michelle Kelly as Mary Poppins in the West End musical.** Photo: Robbie Jack*

*RIGHT: **An actress, costume and false ringlets already in place, starts work on the eyelashes.***

wearing T-shirt, jeans and trainers, he has jumped over a chalk mark on the floor of the rehearsal room and played the scene with no physical problem at all. Now, at the technical rehearsal, he is dressed in tights, tunic and light boots, all of which are close-fitting and designed to make him look smaller and lighter than he is. He must wear, concealed under this apparently flimsy outfit, a stout safety harness from which wire will run, to enable him to 'fly'. High above the Darlings'

nursery set, and well out of sight of the audience, the flymen control the apparatus that enables his flight. There is no magic up there; just precise, technical expertise. Peter must start from an exact point and finish at an exact point. The wire must not distort the costume as he flies or he will look as if he is dangling on a meat hook and the breath-catching moment of magic will be ruined. His boots must not slip as he lands and his little cap must stay in place as he flies through the air. The problems of preventing his wire getting caught on the window frame, or of knocking Wendy flying into the orchestra pit, are, luckily, not within the remit of the Wardrobe.

While the complex problems raised by such moments are sorted out, the actor waits, harnessed, bored, and unable to help; he is unable to do anything, in fact, but fiddle with and worry about his costume. In these moments (or, sometimes, hours) of hanging about, all sorts of costume problems begin to occur. Neckbands itch

and shoes pinch. Skirts feel too long and sleeves too tight.

The tech is the most demanding time in the costume history of a production and it is as well for the designer to be prepared.

THE DRESSING ROOMS

The dressing rooms will have been allotted by the production or stage manager. Each member of the Wardrobe staff will need a copy of the allocation list. Dressers will need to know when the actors they are looking after wear each costume, which accessories go with it, and details of any quick changes. There will be hitches, and the costumes for the final scene may not be ready until just before the scene in which they appear, but the more that can be set in place the better. Actors need time to try on and play in their costumes and to experiment with make-up and hair. The long pauses when technical problems are being solved

Make-shift make-up area and prop store at an open-air production.

134

give actors this time, as they wait to be called onstage. The designer must make sure that any costumes that look alike, such as those for a group of soldiers, are labelled with the name of each actor; when a belt goes missing, it is a help to know whose it is.

Imagine you are an actor coming into an unfamiliar dressing room and seeing your costume and costume props together for the first time. Before this point, the items of clothing and accessories would have been handed to you at fittings. You may not even have seen the fans and shirts and rings. You need first to be sure which are yours and when you are supposed to wear them (is the bonnet for Scene 2 and the cap for Scene 5, or should it be the other way round?), and then to discover how you will look and work in the whole outfit. The Wardrobe should devote time, care and imagination to the arrangement of costumes in the dressing room.

Group each actor's costumes together. Place accessories so that it is clear which hats, shoes, fans, jewellery belong with their costume; the actors can then arrange them as they like and begin to get to know them. When everything actors need to wear or carry is ready in the dressing room, they have tangible proof that you know what you are doing; this confidence in your work will forestall many minor worries that may arise when people have doubts about their costumes. You will be left with more time to deal with the huge flood of questions that erupts at the start of every tech. It is a serious moment for actors when the costume ceases to belong to the Wardrobe and belongs to their character, and this is reflected in the care most actors take to arrange and become familiar with their costumes.

DEALING WITH PROBLEMS

Try to have a helper for the tech, even if you are the only Wardrobe worker for the rest of the time. Being accessible to answer questions during this rehearsal, rather than being safely tucked away in Wardrobe at the top of the building, will make the inevitable list of alterations much shorter; many apparently serious problems may be resolved

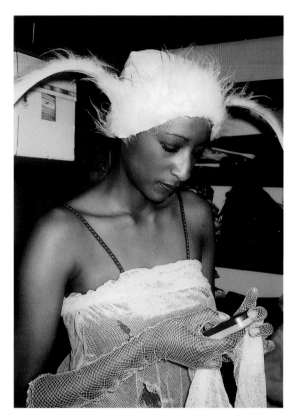

Waiting in costume at the tech.

simply by showing an actor which way round to wear his tunic, or moving a fastening a little to the left or right. These minor hitches take seconds to sort out when the actor is available and wearing the costume, but become more time-consuming if a separate meeting and fitting has to be arranged before the dress rehearsal. Even the most inexperienced helper can write a list of costume problems and be sent out for a pair of inner soles to pad out a shoe or some extra-strong hairspray for a wig.

No Wardrobe worker at the tech should move without a pocketful of safety pins and a notebook and pencil. A basic sewing kit, with small scissors, needles and threads and gaffer tape, will allow the Wardrobe staff to make use of the pauses caused by technical problems onstage by doing minor alterations and marking adjustments on the spot.

135

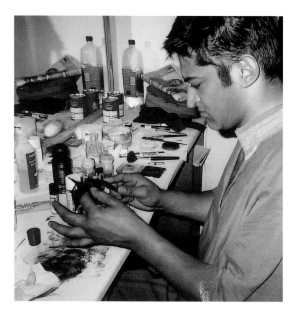

Preparing to attach the beard.

ONSTAGE

The Designer

This will be the first chance a designer has to see the costumes onstage, on people and moving in the light. She will want to see how they look from every part of the auditorium and in every lighting state, and whether the picture they present is the picture in her design. Unless there is a team of makers available, it is a late stage to make any changes, which is why it is important that the progress of making has been checked at fittings. Small changes are possible, but it is advisable to discuss the possibilities for change with the Wardrobe staff before alerting the actor to the fact that you are worried about his costume. Actors may worry, or sometimes become upset, because the picture they see in the mirror is not the picture they have imagined throughout rehearsal. It is difficult for actors to realize that they never see the whole picture presented to the audience. The close-up that they see in the dressing-room mirror is both more detailed and more fragmented than the picture the audience see from the auditorium, when the actor is moving on the set. Designers

need tact and good communication skills to cope when this sort of misunderstanding occurs.

There are occasions when, for one reason or another, a costume is a failure. When this happens, the problem should be addressed firmly and decisively; there is no time to be lost, and recriminations, bad temper or despair do not alter the fact that something has to be done, and quickly. The most consoling thought for a designer is that no one in the audience will mind the substitution of another idea as much as she will, and very few people, even within the company, will be aware of the tornado of work that sweeps the problem away and repairs the disaster. The most important point is to keep the actor's confidence in the costume unimpaired – the quality of their performance is more important than any costume, although that can be hard to remember when you have been up all night sewing on buttons.

The Maker

The maker will be casting a critical eye on her work from the auditorium. It is exciting to see the work finished and enhanced by the lighting, although every maker knows that the slightest fault will glare at the person who made it. If you had difficulty with the set of a collar or the lie of a pocket, that collar or pocket will draw your eye like a magnet. Be reasonable and try and see your work with the eye of the audience rather than a self-critical nit-picker. Note the problems that do need to be addressed – the wavering hemline or slipping shoulder strap – and, unless you have time to spare, ignore the ones that no one but you will notice.

The Designer/Maker/Wardrobe

It is all very well to talk about 'Wardrobe' as if it were a buzzing workroom full of sewing machines and cutting tables, and experienced, calm, helpful people beavering away for the good of the production. The department is much more likely to be a shabby and rather ill-equipped room, housing one or two demented workers, one of whom may be the designer. By half-way through the tech, they may be tearing their thinning hair and rubbing their staring eyes as they add yet more notes to a huge list. However long the list and however urgent the jobs, it is most important that every costume is seen from the auditorium, to check that it looks good onstage. Equally, the dressing rooms must be visited throughout the tech days so that the actors get a chance to talk about any costume worries.

QUICK CHANGES

During the run of the technical rehearsal any quick changes that occur during the action will be rehearsed. The costume department must make sure that these are timed as in the performance. Very quick changes may happen in the wings, to save those vital seconds it would take for the actor to run to the nearest dressing room, and space for these must be arranged with the stage manager. There are a few tips that help quick changes run smoothly:

- Check with actors at fittings the sort of fastenings they prefer and whether they feel safer doing fastenings themselves (at the front) or allowing a dresser or another actor to do them (usually at the back). This will depend whether their hands sweat or shake when they are nervous and on their preference for being in control or being looked after.
- Buttons are reliable and can be larger than on street clothes. It is a natural and unremarkable action to do up a button onstage, unless it is a fly button. The same is not true of Velcro, zips or press studs, which need to be aligned by sight.
- Velcro is quick though noisy to undo, but slow and fiddly to do up neatly.
- Avoid zips. They may be quick, but if they get stuck either up or down, there is no quick repair other than safety pins.
- Time very quick changes in the workroom with a stopwatch, with someone reading the script. It will be useful for the actor and dresser to get to know the change routine in the calm atmosphere and bright light of the Wardrobe rather than in the dim and busy wings during a scene change.

- Work out the best way of laying out the clothes and holding them up for, or passing them to, the actor.
- Make sure that if there is a hold-up onstage during the rehearsal of a quick change that the actor pauses until action resumes. People running the rehearsal from the auditorium tend to forget that an actor and dresser may be timing a change out of sight.
- Changes so quick as to seem almost impossible can be accomplished if actor and dresser learn them like a choreographed dance.
- Quick changes are always slow the first time you try them. Have the confidence to encourage a second attempt before making changes and try to avoid a situation where several people cluster round the actor making suggestions. Stand back and watch the change yourself and suggest any improvements calmly and quietly. Quick changes never work when actors and dresser are flustered and confused.

A pause before an entrance.

137

The List

As the tech progresses the list of jobs to be done before the dress rehearsal grows longer and longer. Once the actors have taken off their costumes, a final list can be made, and the jobs arranged in order of urgency and allotted to the people available to do them. This list may not be as frightening as it appears; many items will be the work of a moment – it takes minutes to take in waist elastic and even less time to ask an actor to emphasize her eyebrows with make-up or wear a hat tilted back on his head. The exhausted Wardrobe crew at the end of the tech feel as if their work – so carefully set out at the beginning of the day – has been reduced to a stirred-up mess and a sweaty muddle. Every comment during the day will have brought news that something is not right. It is very rare for an actor to tell Wardrobe that they are unreservedly happy about their costume. They cannot. It is all too new and must be assimilated into their performance, and everyone else is too involved and busy to talk about anything that does not present an immediate problem. The list calms and orders the chaos and prevents jobs being overlooked, but it has another, less tangible, effect, which is just as important. Crossing things off the list raises the spirits and proves to everyone that the work is under control. Never under-estimate the morale-raising power of a whole page of crossed-off jobs.

The Dress Rehearsal

The costumes should all be ready and finished in the dressing rooms – the actors will have got used to wearing them during the tech – and everything is ready for the dress rehearsal. At least that what it is supposed to be like, but there are times when the King does not get his crown until just before his entrance, or the court jester is wearing his own trainers because his boots have not arrived, or he developed a blister during the long-drawn-out tech. The dress rehearsal, if all runs smoothly, will be an exact pattern of the first-night show, but without an audience. Instead of the paying public enjoying the show, the directors, designers and those members of the crew who are not needed onstage will be seeing their work as the audience will see it. The collage of lights and sound, set and costume all comes together for the first time and the result of those early production meetings, when ideas were first discussed, are seen and heard onstage. Despite the tugging nerves because of the nearness of the first night, it is an exciting occasion. The costume crew forget their exhaustion and remember why they wanted to work with theatre costumes and why they go on doing it.

There is no possible reason to do such a demanding job unless you really do love it. And if you do love it, there are few jobs that give such concrete and varied satisfaction, even though you are usually galloping in a panting sprint of work towards this finishing line of the dress rehearsal. After all, how many jobs give you the opportunity to imagine a picture, make it come true, and see it come to life in front of your eyes in the magical stage light? When things go wrong, it is gloomy and lonely, but when it works, when you see the confidence that your costumes have inspired in the cast, when you know the picture you have created is giving the right messages to the audience, and when you see the pictures in your mind brought to life by the actors, it feels like the luckiest job in the world.

APPENDIX: JARGON-BUSTER

This list contains some terms and slang and phrases that are heard in and around theatres. The beginner in the wardrobe will hear phrases or words that appear to make no sense at all. Most of them do not relate particularly to costume, but all are heard often in the costume department, and it's useful to know what they mean. There are hundreds of others, and actors and technicians of different ages use different slang. More complete sources of information can be found in the bibliography.

accident book the management is obliged to keep a record of any accidents in the building

ASM Assistant Stage Manager

baldric a belt, usually worn over one shoulder to hold a sword, a musical instrument etc.

band room the band's dressing room

beginners five minutes before the performance starts

bible (in the wardrobe) the file of designs containing fabric swatches, actor's measurements and all information relevant to the costumes

black light ultra-violet (UV) light

blackout when all the lights go out on-stage

blacks the black clothes the stage management and anybody else who might be glimpsed by a member of the audience wear during performances

bling costume jewellery and glamour-glitter

bodge, bodging rescuing a piece of work that has gone wrong by un-orthodox means, as in secreting a layer of glue on the back of a fraying buttonhole

book ('the book') where the script and every cue and action in the show is written down

break a pause in rehearsals, or the end of rehearsals as in 'have they broken yet?'

breaking down a costume making it look old and worn

breeks breeches

calls information for the company about rehearsals or performance

change in the wings a quick change that takes place on the side of the stage

cod pretend, as in 'cod truncheon' – a truncheon that would not hurt when whacked on a head!

comps free tickets

costume prop a prop, such as a handkerchief, which is part of the costume

crin-wire stiff steel or heavy plastic wire used to support a crinoline

dark no performance, as in 'the theatre is dark on Monday.'

double a duplicate costume, an actor playing two roles, two actors playing one role.

downstage stage area nearest the audience

drape a curtain hanging on stage

dress call, dress parade actors in costume pre-dress rehearsal for the purpose of checking by the costume department that all is well, and showing the director and the rest of the company what the costumes will look like

dress run a rehearsal in costume

dresser someone who helps the actors to get into their costumes and with their costume changes

139

DSM Deputy Stage Manager

falsies false breasts

fire code a code phrase that is used by the company as a fire warning that will not cause panic in the audience as in 'Mr Red is in the house tonight.'

five ('the five') ten minutes before the performance starts as in 'This is your five minute call'

flies area above the stage

focusing adjusting the lighting

frocks male or female costumes

front of house any part of the theatre open to the public

gaffer, gaffer tape very sticky wide plastic tape, usually black, white or silver; also used as a verb – 'gaffer it down', meaning 'stick it down'

gel the transparent film that colours stage lighting

general cover a wash of light over the whole stage

glover's needle a needle with blades for sewing leather and tough fabric

'going to black' a warning that the lights onstage are going out and no-one should move

gongs medals

green room the actors' sitting room

half ('the half') thirty-five minutes before the performance starts, as in 'Have they called the half?' 'Have we had the half?' – has the Stage Manager informed the company that there are thirty-five minutes until the performance starts

harness the straps round the body to which mechanism for flying an actor is attached

heel grips rubber slips glued on the inside of the heel of the shoe to prevent shoe slipping

hoofer dancer

hose men's tights or stockings

house the audience

house seats seats kept back by the management for unexpected VIPs

juveniles, juves child performers

Kensington gore stage blood

line run a rehearsal of the words without movement

luck some actors consider real flowers onstage, whistling, or saying 'Macbeth' or 'good luck' backstage, unlucky; these are the most common of many backstage superstitions.

LX short for electrics, lighting

mattress needle a large eyed, long , curved needle

notes a time after each rehearsal and some performances when the company gathers for the director's comment on the work

Number 1 dressing room the dressing room nearest the stage

onstage change a costume change which happens onstage

out front in the audience

paint shop where scenery is painted

pass door the door between front of house and backstage

personal prop a prop that is looked after by the actor in his dressing room rather than set at the side of the stage

photo call rehearsal, performance or organised event when photographs will be taken (often requiring actors in costume)

plotting deciding or marking down actors' moves, lighting and sound cues and changes, etc

practical something that must really do its job, such as a handbag that has to be opened on stage rather than just be carried

practical pocket a pocket that will have to be used in the course of the stage action

press call publicity event

prompt corner the area, usually stage left, from which the stage manager controls the running of the performance

prop object an object that has to look right on stage but need not work, such as a lighter which is carried but never used to light a cigarette

pulling choosing costumes from stock

QC (written) short for quick change

quarter ('the quarter') twenty minutes before the performance starts

rigging (noun) the mechanisms for moving and holding scenery and lights

rigging (verb) putting up the lights

scene dock where scenery is stored and sometimes painted

'Scottish play' *Macbeth*

show report a report written by the stage management of any exceptional happening during a performance

show socks, show pants, etc underwear provided and washed by the wardrobe

skip a big wicker basket for transporting costumes and props

slap make-up

slosh, slosh scene a scene when costumes will get wet and messy

SM Stage Manager

sparks electrician

spot a limited area of light

stage left the left-hand side of the stage from the actor's, not the audience's, point of view

stage right the right-hand side of the stage from the actor's, not the audience's, point of view

stagger through a very early rehearsal of the whole play

stand-in a person, prop or costume that takes the place of the real person or thing

stays corsets

tabs stage curtains

tannoy the loud-speaker system that relays what's happening on stage, and the Stage Manager's calls, to the rest of the theatre and dressing rooms

taps the metal bits on tap-shoes

tarting up a costume cleaning it up, making it look smarter: 'It'll look ok when we've tarted it up'

tat sequins, braid, lace and other decoration on a costume

tatting up a costume decorating it

tech run a rehearsal for the technical aspects of the show rather than the acting

techie backstage worker

test light a stage light rigged up in the wardrobe to try out the effect of light on fabric

timing a change running through the lines and action which take place during a quick change

toupee tape double-sided sticky tape for attaching wigs shoulder straps, etc., to heads and bodies

upstage stage areas furthest away from the audience

warm-up a period before the show for performers to prepare their bodies and voices for performance

wig block a head-shaped stand to store wigs on

wing it to invent, decide or improvise at the last moment

wings area of the stage that the audience can't see

BIBLIOGRAPHY

Arnold, J., *Patterns of Fashion 1560–1620* (Macmillan, 1985) ISBN 0333382946

Arnold, J., *Patterns of Fashion 1960–1920* (Macmillan, 1977) ISBN 0333136017

Bicât, T., *Making Stage Costumes* (Crowood, 2001) ISBN 1861264089

Bicât, T., *Period Costume for the Stage* (Crowood, 2003) ISBN 1861265891

Bicât, T., *Pantomime* (Crowood, 2004) ISBN 1861266928

Boucher, F., *A History of Costume in the West* (Thames and Hudson) ISBN 0500014167

Camp, Carole Ann, *The Complete Idiot's Guide to Sewing* (Penguin Group, 2005) ISBN 0028638913

Cumming, V., *The Visual History of Costume Accessories* (Batsford, 1998) ISBN 0713473754

Dial, Tim, *Basic Millinery for the Stage* (Heineman, 2002) ISBN 032500336X

Doyle, R., *Waisted Efforts – An Illustrated Guide to Corset Making* (Sartorial Press Publications, 1997) ISBN 09683033900

Motley, *Designing and Making Stage Costumes* (Taylor & Francis Books, 1992) ISBN 1871569443

Nunn, J., *Fashion in Costume* (A&C Black, 2000) ISBN 0713650036

Swinfield, R., *Stage Make-up Step by Step* (A&C Black, 1995) ISBN 0713642092

Thorne, Gary, *Designing Stage Costumes* (Crowood, 2000) ISBN 186126416X

Waugh, N., *The Cut of Men's Clothes* (Faber & Faber, 1994) ISBN 0571057144

Waugh, N., *The Cut of Women's Clothes* (Faber & Faber, 1994) ISBN 0571085946

INDEX

INDEX